The Globalization of Higher Education

Edited by
Peter Scott

The Society for Research into Higher Education
& Open University Press

Published by SRHE and
Open University Press
Celtic Court
22 Ballmoor   64182
Buckingham
MK 18 1XW

email: enquiries@openup.co.uk
world wide web: http://www.openup.co.uk

and 325 Chestnut Street
Philadelphia, PA 19106, USA

First published 1998

A catalogue record of this book is available from the British Library

ISBN 0 335 20244 6 (pb)   0 335 20245 4 (hb)

Library of Congress Cataloging-in-Publication Data

The globalization of higher education/edited by Peter Scott.
    p.   cm.
    'Proceedings of the 1998 Annual Conference of the Society for
Research into Higher Education at Lancaster University' – Pref.
    Includes bibliographical references and index.
    ISBN 0–335–20245–4 (hardcover). – ISBN 0–335–20244–6 (pbk.)
    1. Education, Higher – Aims and objectives – Congresses.
2. International education – Congresses.   3. Intellectual
cooperation – Congresses.   I. Scott, Peter, 1946– .   II. Society
for Research into Higher Education. Conference (1998: Lancaster
University)
LB2322.2.G56   1998
378 – dc21
                            378 Sco   98–27036
                                                         CIP

Typeset by Graphicraft Limited, Hong Kong
Printed in Great Britain by St Edmundsbury Press Ltd,
Bury St Edmunds, Suffolk

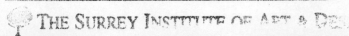

Contents

Contributors

Alison Barty is counsellor with special responsibility for international students at South Bank University. Previously she was Deputy Executive Secretary at UKCOSA.

Professor Clive Booth is chairman of the Teacher Training Agency, a vice-president of the Society for Research into Higher Education and a senior adviser to the British Council. He was formerly vice-chancellor of Oxford Brookes University.

Tom Bruch is Secretary General of the Lutheran Council of Great Britain and was formerly Director of Advice and Training at UKCOSA: the Council for International Education.

Hilary Callan is director of the European Association for International Education.

David Elliott is in charge of the British Council's office in Israel, and was formerly head of higher education at the Council.

Professor Michael Gibbons is secretary-general of the Association of Commonwealth Universities, and was formerly director of the Science Policy Research Unit at the University of Sussex.

Roshen Kishun is president of the International Education Association of South Africa, and deputy registrar at the University of Natal in Durban.

Jan Sadlak is head of higher education policy at UNESCO (United Nations Educational, Scientific and Cultural Organization) in Paris.

Peter Scott is vice-chancellor of Kingston University and was chairman of UKCOSA's executive committee from 1992 to 1998.

Professor Ulrich Teichler is director of the Wissenschaftliches Zentrum für Berufs-und Hochschulforschung at the University of Kassel and also a vice-president of the Society for Research into Higher Education.

Professor John Urry is professor of sociology at Lancaster University.

Preface

From its first beginnings the university was a 'universal' institution rooted in the unity of Western Christendom. In the age of European empires, and of imperial science, it became an international institution. In the late twentieth century, with the emergence of a Knowledge Society, it is about to become a global institution. This book, which forms the precedings of the 1998 annual conference of the Society for Research into Higher Education at Lancaster University and shares the same theme, is an attempt to make sense of the prospects of global change now facing higher education.

The book begins with John Urry's wide-ranging analysis of changing conceptions of time and space in the (post?) modern world. Chapters 2 and 3 explore the processes of internationalization within British higher education – but from different perspectives. Tom Bruch and Alison Barty offer a users' and institutional perspective, while David Elliott (with an afterword by Clive Booth) provides an account of policy developments. The British experience of internationalization is then complemented by two other accounts: in Chapter 4 Hilary Callan discusses the approaches of other European countries and in Chapter 5 Roshen Kishun describes South African higher education's encounter with the wider world. The next three chapters are concerned with supranational perspectives on the internationalization of higher education. In Chapter 6 Michael Gibbons discusses the Commonwealth's contribution to globalization; in Chapter 7 Ulrich Teichler analyses the European Union's increasingly significant role; and in Chapter 8 Jan Sadlak offers a UNESCO (United Nations Educational, Scientific and Cultural Organization) perspective on the worldwide challenges facing higher education. Finally in Chapter 9 Peter Scott discusses the tensions between massification, internationalization and globalization.

Peter Scott

1

Contemporary Transformations of Time and Space

John Urry

There is no such thing as society.

(Margaret Thatcher)

In much current literature there is said to be a death of the human subject. A wide variety of discourses and disciplines have problematized the role of human subjects and their apparently unique powers to create and sustain distinctive patterns of human life. Some examples of these discourses which have made the future of the human questionable include post-structuralist analyses of the death of the author/subject; anthropology's interrogation of 'cyborg cultures'; analyses of the implications for the human of prosthetic technologies; the development of a sociology and anthropology of material objects; the more general application of actor network theory from the sociology of science; the social science interest in the growing riskiness of waste and the physical environment and the threats this presents to the future of the human species; analyses of the partially independent effects of time and space; sociobiological attacks on dualistic notions of mind and body; the post-modern critique of metanarratives of human redemption; and the implications for the human-social world of recent chaos and complexity theories.

This battery of claims must make us wonder whether there is anything left which is specifically human. Do humans retain powers to realize outcomes which are in some sense species-specific? Is there a human subject? This chapter addresses these issues somewhat obliquely. My concern is two-fold. First, I consider the notion of the social and particularly whether a range of transformations of time and space have problematized the very idea of the social and the claim that social relationships between people have the power in themselves to generate and hence to explain significant phenomena.

Second, I consider the concept of the bounded society. Is this notion coherent? Are there, empirically, such bounded societies? Societies are typically presumed to be sovereign social entities with a State at the centre which organizes the rights and duties of each member. Most major sets of social relationships are seen as flowing within the territorial boundaries of each society. The State possesses a monopoly of jurisdiction over the territory of the society. It is presumed that especially economies, but also politics, culture, classes, gender and so on, are societally structured. In combination such relations constitute the social structure in terms of which the life chances of each member of that society are organized and regulated. Moreover, through their interdependence with each other, all societies are constituted as self-regulating entities significantly defined by their differences from other societies. What I term the North Atlantic rim (North America and Western Europe) has been constituted as a system of such national societies, with clear boundaries that mark off one society from another (Held 1995; Rose 1996).

Moreover, the concept of society has been central to Western notions over the past two centuries of what it is to be a human being, especially a human possessing the rights and duties of citizenship. To be human has meant that one is unambiguously a member of a particular society. Historically and conceptually there has been a strong connection between the idea of humanness and that of membership of a society. Society is taken here not in the general civilizational sense but as ordered through a nation-state, with clear territorial and citizenship boundaries and a system of governance over its particular citizens. Conceptually and historically there has been an indivisible duality, of humans and of (human) societies. Each has not and could not exist without the other.

Furthermore, this notion of society implied a very strong distinction from that of nature, whether or not that pre-social nature was viewed as Hobbesian or Lockean. Nature was viewed as, and degraded into, a realm of unfreedom and hostility that needed to be subdued and controlled. Modernity involved the belief that human progress should be measured and evaluated in terms of the domination of nature rather than through transforming the relationship between 'humans' and 'nature'. This view that nature is fundamentally separate from and to be dominated by human societies presupposed the doctrine of human exceptionalism: that humans are fundamentally different from and superior to all other species; that people can determine their own destinies and learn whatever is necessary to achieve them; that the world is vast and presents unlimited opportunities for the human race; and that the history of human society is one of unending progress.

But in recent years various writers, as I indicated in the first paragraph, have problematized this distinction (Haraway 1991; Latour 1993; Michael 1996). There is, it is argued, a striking leakiness of distinctions and a need to transcend most of the ways in which the specifically human and the natural have been represented and sustained (Strathern 1992). The 'natural' or 'nature' is a particular thorn in the side of any argument which presumes that there is something specific about the social-cum-societal levels of analysis. In particular the debates on risk have involved a conceptualization of a particular type of society: a risk as opposed to an industrial society. Risk societies are those organized around the dangerous flows of human waste and of their consequences which result from treating the globe as a laboratory (Beck 1992). In such societies Beck argues that risks have become incalculable, uncompensatable, unlimited, unaccountable and, most important of all, invisible to our senses. The paradigm case of such invisible risks is that of nuclear radiation, a risk which cannot be directly touched, tasted, heard, smelt and especially seen. As Beck argues about Chernobyl:

> We look, we listen further, but the normality of our sensual perception deceives. In the face of this danger, our senses fail us. All of us . . . were blinded even when we saw. We experienced a world, unchanged for our senses, behind which a hidden contamination and danger occurred that was closed to our view.
>
> (cited in Adam 1995: 11)

Beck argues that particular kinds of society develop on the basis of this disempowerment of the senses and of the awesome effects of the globalization of such risks upon human life. Hence the globalization of and the transformation of nature risk alters the very character of society. Many of the differences between them are eroded through the development of risks that know no national borders and which subject everyone to their insensible power, although much 'cultural work' is still necessary in order that peoples come to see that they do in fact face common global problems (Wynne 1994). These processes would be better described as involving the development of a 'risk culture' rather than a 'risk society' since the latter term suggests that there is no change in the powers of bounded societies (see below).

Three conclusions follow from this brief consideration of the inhuman. First, developments which are massively significant for humans with regard to technology, science, the body, nature and the environment do not derive from specifically human intentions and actions (see Murdoch 1995 on the importance of the inhuman with regard to economic change). There are no *social* structures either in the sense of social interactions of presence and absence, or in the sense of enduring social relations which people bear. Both kinds of formulation of the social omit the power of the inhuman.

Second, the kind of metaphor appropriate to capture this growing complexity of peoples and objects is that of the network, the web, or the flow, not that of structure. The latter implies a centre, hierarchy and constitution. Castells, in *The Rise of the Network Society* has recently elaborated on how human life is 'increasingly structured around a bipolar opposition between the Net and the Self' (Castells 1996: 3). But 'Net' here does not mean social networks but involves complex and enduring connections between peoples, technologies and things (Murdoch 1995: 745).

Third, these networks can spread across time and space, whereas according to Law: 'left to their own devices human actions and words do not spread very far at all' (Law 1994: 24). Different networks thus possess different reaches or abilities to bring home distant events, places or people (Latour

1987; Murdoch 1995). Accountancy is particularly effective at reducing the variety of activities at distant places into a common set of figures that can be instantaneously translated back to other parts of the network. But more generally, the development of various global flows transforms the constraints and opportunities which face individual humans, and in particular locates people and objects in novel networks. These appear to shift from being those of 'national societies' based upon a given social structure, to globalizing flows or networks of signs, money, information, technologies, machines, waste products, as well as people (Lash and Urry 1994). Such global flows criss-cross national borders disrupting the apparently organized coherence of individual national societies and generating new unexpected networks or webs of connections between peoples and objects. This shift explains why it has been argued that we do not so much inhabit a risk society with its implied fixities of institution and social structure, but rather an indeterminant, ambivalent and semiotic risk culture where the risks are in part generated by the declining powers of national societies in the face of 'inhuman' global flows and multiple networks (Lash 1995).

Inhuman globalization

It was a characteristic of what I call organized capitalism (roughly 1900s–1970s in Europe and North America) that most economic and social problems or risks were thought to be produced by and soluble at the level of the individual society. The concerns of each were to be dealt with through national policies, especially through a Keynesian welfare state which could identify and respond to the risks of organized capitalism (Lash and Urry 1987, 1994). These risks were seen as principally located *within* the borders of each society, and solutions were also envisaged as devised and implemented within such national borders. National societies were based upon a concept of the citizen who owed duties to and received rights from their society through the core institutions of the nation-state (Held 1995; Rose 1996).

However, this 'societal' model only really applied to the dozen or so societies of the North Atlantic rim – and even here the Vatican in Rome partially dominated the domestic policies of a number of 'southern' European countries (Walby 1996). Most of the rest of the world was subject to colonial domination, and it was the societies of the North Atlantic rim which were themselves mainly the colonial powers, having hugely significant economic, military, social and especially cultural relationships beyond their borders. Moreover, one particular national society, Germany, was nearly able to subject most of 'Europe' to its military hegemony, while for much of the twentieth century the most powerful society, the USA, has principally functioned as a superpower locked into an escalating diplomatic, political, military, economic and cultural struggle with another massively powerful imperial society, the former Soviet Union.

However, whatever the limits of the 'societal' model, there do seem to have developed an extraordinary array of processes which undermine whatever had remained of a societal conceptualization of what it was to be a human being at the end of the twentieth century. I will begin by noting a variety of different discourses which have created a huge academic and popular literature on such topics. According to figures assembled by Busch (1997) the number of articles with 'globalization/global' in the title has increased almost threefold in the past decade.

First, there is a burgeoning academic discourse focused around the analysis of global flows which individual nation-states seem relatively powerless to resist and which clearly disrupt a variety of nationally organized structures and programmes (Held 1993; Lash and Urry 1994). Such flows also involve the remaking of local as well as global relations. Second, there is the sense of the term 'global' as an ideology. This notion is employed by those with interests in promoting worldwide capitalist relations and undermining national identity and the kinds of social democratic project that such identities underlie and authorize (Ohmae 1990). These processes appear to be producing a new global epoch which is for Ohmae producing a new golden age of 'borderlessness'. The term 'global' may also refer to the kinds of strategies employed by transnational corporations which involve a lack of commitment to particular territories, labour forces or governments. Also, 'global' may refer to the basis of political mobilization – the cultural construction of an issue as global provides greater resources for mobilization and resistance across a much wider range of individuals and organizations. This can be seen in the way that both environmental change and media domination are now constructed as global (Wynne 1994). Further, the notion of the global can refer to images employed in advertising, environmentalism, political discourse and so on, as in the 'blue earth' or the 'fragile earth'. Such an image may be employed to sell products, ideas or further images, and can be deployed by both commercial and non-governmental/organisational interests. Finally, globalization is sometimes taken to refer to a new mediaevalism characterized by competing institutions with overlapping jurisdictions and identities; states reconstituted as competition-states; the emergence of various empires, including those of Microsoft and Coca-Cola; the absence of external threat for many nation-states; the development of transnational regions; and the growth of city-states (Cerny 1997).

Let us now consider some key processes which develop global networks (the examples below are drawn from the extensive literature, notably Appadurai 1990; Brunn and Leinbach 1991; Gilroy 1993; Lash and Urry 1994; Featherstone *et al.* 1995; Waters 1985; Albrow 1996; Castells 1996; Eade 1997.)

Global networks have been dramatically affected by the development of new machines and technologies which shrink time-space and in part at least transcend societal control and regulation. These include fibre-optic cables, jet planes, audio-visual transmissions, digital TV, computer networks including the Internet, satellites, credit cards, faxes, electronic point-of-sale terminals, portable phones, electronic stock exchanges, high speed trains and virtual reality. There are also large increases in nuclear, chemical and conventional military technologies and weapons, as well as new waste products and health risks, which necessitate inter-societal regulation to ensure personal and national security.

Such machines and technologies are organized in terms of various *scapes*. These are the networks of machines, technologies, organizations, texts and actors along which the various flows can be relayed. An example of such a scape is the network of hub airports which structure the global flows of the 500 million or so international travellers each year. The flows consist of not just of the flows of people, but also of images, information, money, technologies and waste that are moved within and especially across national borders and which individual societies are unable or unwilling to control. Once particular scapes have been established then individuals and especially corporations within each society will mostly endeavour to become connected to them, such as developing a hub airport, being plugged into the Internet, attracting satellite broadcasting and even reprocessing nuclear waste products. The development of these networked scapes creates new inequalities of access/non-access which do not map onto the jurisdictions of particular societies (see the journal *Space as Culture*, vol. *1*, part 1).

Aesthetic images and informational signs are particularly significant scapes and flows which exemplify the time–space compression of the global world. There are massively powerful cultural industries, which produce and market images, both to advertise commercial products and to promote peoples, states, NGOs (non-governmental organizations), places, universities and so on (including the very image of the 'one earth'). Images are also increasingly themselves products, and this is particularly important within the multimedia which serve to constitute various economies of images. There are also the various scapes along which extraordinary amounts of information flows (e.g. financial, economic, scientific and news data) into which some groups are extremely well plugged but from which others are effectively excluded.

Certain scapes have become partially organized at the global level. Organizations responsible for facilitating the globalization of scapes and citizenship include the United Nations (UN), the World Bank, Microsoft, CNN, Greenpeace, the European Union (EU), News International, the Oscar ceremony, the World Intellectual Property Organisation, the United Nations Educational, Scientific and Cultural Organization (UNESCO), the Olympic movement, Friends of the Earth, Nobel prizes, Band-Aid, the Brundtland Report, the Rio Earth Summit, the European Court of Human Rights, the British Council and so on. These employ most if not all of the machines and technologies listed above.

These scapes generate, for late twentieth-century 'humans', new opportunities and desires, as well as new risks. The former include cheap overseas travel; forming internationalized 'new sociations', especially via the Internet; obtaining consumer goods and lifestyles of 'the other'; employing global imagery; participating in global cultural events; listening to 'world music'; and so on. The latter includes AIDS; Chernobyl; cultural homogenization; the loss of economic national sovereignty; migration; being exiled; and asylum seeking. These 'global' patterns can be described as the hollowing out of existing societies, especially as a plethora of 'sociations' have developed, concerned to reflect upon, to argue against, to retreat from, to provide alternatives to and to campaign for, these various scapes and flows. This generates within any existing 'society' a complex, overlapping, disjunctive order of off-centredness as these multiple flows are chronically combined and recombined across times and spaces often unrelated to the boundaries of existing societies and often following a kind of hypertextual patterning. Notions of mobility and flow are seen as constitutive of identity which is less societal and more defined in terms of consuming elements of one or more of the putatively global scapes, so forming or reinforcing new networks.

The widespread flows across societal borders makes it less easy for states to mobilize clearly separate and coherent nations in pursuit of societal goals. This can be seen both economically and culturally. In terms of the former, the breaking down of the coherence of 'national economies' has been combined with an increased political unwillingness of many states to tax and spend let alone to nationalize industries so as to bring them under societal control. States have increasingly shifted to a regulative rather than a direct production/employment function, partly facilitated by new forms of information gathering, storage and retrieval. In many ways the EU is the quintessential regulatory state. In terms of the latter, the hybridization of cultures, the global refugee problem, the importance of travelling cultures, some growth of a global dwellingness, diasporas and other notions of the 'unhomely' all problematize the notion of a society which is somehow in and of itself able to mobilize for action. These configurations weaken the power of the societal to draw together its citizens as one, to govern in its unique name, to endow all with national identity and to speak with a single voice. As Rose argues, while 'our political, professional, moral and cultural authorities still speak happily of "society", the very meaning and ethical salience of this term is under question as "society" is perceived as dissociated into a variety of ethical and cultural communities with incompatible allegiances and incommensurable obligations' (Rose 1996: 353).

The consequences of these developing global processes are multiple, overlapping and disjunctive. In some writings the globalization thesis is an attempted reassertion of a modernist metanarrative which involves the claim that global markets generate economic, political and cultural homogenization. In the following discussion, however, I presume no such necessary homogenization. Taylor (1997) usefully notes that constructing a noun out of a verb by adding 'ization' creates a peculiar double meaning in the English language. The new word, such as 'modernization' or 'globalization' provides a term for both the process described by the verb (to modernize, to globalize) and a term apparently characterizing the end-state of that process. This is deeply confusing. Hence it is important to distinguish between globalization

...d globalization as 'hypothesis', as well as between globalization
...ess and globalization as 'discourse', and between economic/
...d cultural/environmental globalizations. Thus in Hirst and
...'s recent effort to refute the thesis of globalization they treat
...ion as outcome, as real process, and as economic/political. They
have ...de difficulty in refuting such a simplistic modernist argument and
hence in showing that there are still things that nation-states can do, especially to form treaties and international regulations. However, in the next
section I take globalization to be not an outcome but a hypothesis. For
me, it is importantly both a description of putatively real processes and of
certain kinds of discourse, and should be viewed as being as much cultural/
environmental as it is economic/political.

There is though one further issue here, namely whether the process of
globalization is thought to produce homogenous outcomes (such as the
supposed 'cocacolonization' of the world) or strongly increased diversity
(through the increased significance of the 'local'). In different writings
both have been treated as evidence of supposed 'globalization'. In the case
of the latter this occurs through the multiple ways in which it is claimed
that the global may combine with particular local processes, generating the
so-called 'glocal' effects. Indeed the more we are concerned with globalization as culture, the more significant are these global-local combinations
and the less clear-cut are the empirical indicators of a simple 'globalization-as-
outcome-thesis'.

Global networks

I shall consider four exemplars which in their different ways bring out the
power of these inhuman global networks which increasingly criss-cross
national borders. The first to be considered here is that of the French
Minitel computer system contrasted with the American Arpanet/Internet
systems. The global dominance of the latter within the 1990s reflects the
shift from societal to putatively global networks (Castells 1996, especially
Chapter 5). The videotext Minitel system is based within the borders of
France and resulted from initiatives by the French State to develop its
domestic electronic industries. It started in the mid-1980s and by the
mid-1990s was used by one-third of the French population. Each French
household was offered a free Minitel terminal (based on limited video and
transmission technology) instead of the usual telephone book. Many business
and other services became available on the Minitel, including sex chat lines.
Minitel was thus established as a national system organized by the French
nation-state, and based on the ordered character of the telephone book
and homogenous tariffs wherever one lived in France.

However, by the mid-1990s Minitel's technology was proving out of date.
Its terminals were not those of normal computer systems. Also the system's
architecture was based upon a hierarchy of server networks and this meant

that it had little capacity for horizontal communication. In the end it became necessary to provide a way of linking these terminals (at a price) to the international Internet, and this is now available. Minitel has thus become yet another network plugged into the ungoverned, anarchic and generalized system of the Internet which links at least 44,000 networks with possibly 30 million users worldwide.

Arpanet/Internet began as a military-based computer system in the USA designed to enable communications to continue in the event of a nuclear attack. This was achieved through developing a network which was independent of command and control centres, message units being able to find their own routes in packages along the network. Its development into the global Internet was not simply the result of initiatives from the military and then from American scientific and research networks, but also stemmed from the more counter-cultural efforts to produce a computer network with universal public access. For example, students were responsible for 'inventing' the modem in 1978 and the Web browser Mosaic in 1992. These were key moments in the development of a personal computing counter-culture. As Castells notes: 'the openness of the system also results from the constant process of innovation and free accessibility enacted by early computer hackers and the network hobbyists who still populate the net by the thousands' (1996: 356). The Internet has developed into a system enabling horizontal global communication which is very hard to control or censor by national or indeed international States. The Internet is in many ways the metaphor for networked globalization at the end of the twentieth century, involving thousands of networks of people, machines, programmes, texts and images in which there are quasi-subjects and quasi-objects.

The second and quite different example is the significance of various networks in relationship to the collapse of communist State regimes in what used to be known as 'Eastern Europe'. My comments here will be very general and schematic (see Braun *et al.* 1996). Following the Second World War the individual societies of Central and Eastern Europe constructed exceptionally strong frontiers, both from the 'West' and most strikingly from each other. Cultural communication into and out of such societies was exceptionally difficult: the Cold War chilled culture as well as politics. So although such societies were internationally linked via the hegemony of the former Soviet Union (economically via COMECON, the pact for mutual economic co-operation, and politically/militarily via the Warsaw Pact), there was a parallel emphasis upon cultural involution and the reinforcement of national distinctiveness.

What is increasingly clear is that frontiers of this sort were there to be transgressed. The attempt to maintain or perhaps to freeze the peoples and cultures of 'Eastern Europe' simply could not succeed. The Berlin wall was of course the most stunning example of this attempted preservation of the peoples of a society. However, through the 1960s forms of communication and later of leisure travel did in fact increase. Both peoples and especially objects began to flow across the carefully constructed borders, often involving what has been termed the 'invisible hand of the smuggler' (Braun *et al.* 1996: 1). Such objects especially of the 'West' became used and talked about in multiple informal ways, helping the citizens of such societies to form new bases of personal identity, new ways of collectively remembering and new images of self and society. Many citizens went to inordinate lengths to learn about and to acquire objects that seemingly represented Western taste. Because there was little chance to develop identity within work or politics, it is suggested that many people poured their energies into high and low culture and especially the material objects which in one way or another symbolized or captured such an identity. Braun *et al.* (1996: 2) argue that these 'socially constructed desires did, in fact, play a larger role in the implosion of state socialist systems of Europe than any political ideology'.

In particular these east European economies had been organized around the primacy of industrial production and the restriction of consumer demand, somewhat akin to the relative short-term austerity of wartime in the 'West'. But such restrictions upon the scale and variety of consumption were not freely assented to; indeed the more restricted the choices, especially by comparison with what appeared to be happening in the 'West', the more importance consumer goods or their substitutes acquired both for individuals and for various social networks. Hence modes of 'shopping tourism' developed on a mass scale and resulted in the arrival of objects in these countries which were then often sold on through networks and which further raised people's expectations of the wealth and consumer riches of the 'West'. Such objects constituted significant cultural markers. Braun *et al.* (1996: 6) argue that the multiple network-organized movements of people in search of various material objects was a key feature of societies in which barriers to consumption were constituted as official State policy.

There are a number of ways in which objects thus functioned within the history of the present of Eastern Europe: there was simply a fascination with consumer goods, with distinctions of style and taste and more broadly with shopping as an intensely pleasurable activity; there was a process of generating 'cult' products such as American jogging shoes or Western books; there was a more general belief that the 'West' set the standard for what was appropriately 'classy'; travel to other countries and especially to the 'West' always involved extensive purchases of consumer goods for family members, but especially to sell on to others; and there was also extensive smuggling of goods by tourists, lorry drivers and others who used social networks on their return to sell their goods which marked out the sophistication of the 'West' and the presumed failure of the 'East'. The social networks of shoppers, tourists, travellers, black marketers, smugglers and so on combined with particular consumer objects and modes of transportation to bring down these 'societies' which did not have the social power to stem the inevitable march of goods, services, signs, images and people across what had been some of the most powerfully policed of national borders.

The third example concerns the paradoxical consequence of globalization of engendering multiple forms of opposition to its various effects. Many groups and associations are energized by passionate opposition to many of the institutions of the new global order. Globalization, in other words, generates its opposition, although there is little or no agreement on the causes and consequences of global disorder. Such a resistant order to global institutions is highly fragmented and disparate, and includes, for example: the Zapatistas in Mexico; the American Militia and the Patriots more generally; Aum Shinrikyo in Japan; many environmental NGOs; the women's movement concerned with the impacts of the global market-place upon women and children in developing countries; New Ageists; religious fundamentalist groups; and so on (Castells 1997). All oppose aspects of the new global order; and yet partly through their practices they serve to 'de-totalize' each society. They are all virtual communities which 'exist only to the extent that their constituents are linked together through identifications constructed in the non-geographic spaces of activist discourses, cultural products and media images' (Rose 1996: 333).

And yet, such networks routinely employ the machines and technologies of the global order. Castells terms the Zapatistas the 'first informational guerrillas' since they particularly deploy computer mediated communication and the establishment of a global electronic network of solidarity groups (Castells 1997, Chapter 3). Similar widespread use of the Internet is to be found among the American Patriots who believe that the Federal State is turning the USA into a part of the global economy and destroying American sovereignty. They particularly oppose Federal attempts to regulate the environment, as opposed to the sustaining of local customs and culture. There are therefore very varied networks produced – networks of people and objects often mediated through various kinds of consumer purchase. Burgess (1990: 144) writes of new forms of global cultural politics which focus upon the Amazonian rainforest: 'the alliance between actors, musicians, Brazilian Indians, population music promoters, conservation organisations, the media industry and mainly young consumers who buy records to support the campaign against the destruction of the Amazonian rainforest'.

This relates more generally to changes taking place in what it is to be a 'member' of various organizations in the emergent global age. Membership has typically been thought of in terms of joining organizations which then provide various rights and duties to their members, and these are organized through a hierarchy. Trade unions were the classic model of this. But what has happened is that new 'organizations' have developed which are much more *media*-ted, Greenpeace being the classic example of an oppositional organization exceptionally skilled at developing and handling its media images (see Szerszynski 1997). So although part of its appeal is through the bearing of witness and the transgressive use of theatre, metaphor and symbol, Greenpeace mainly constructs its membership as relatively passive 'supporters'. Thus while it is the bearer of ecological wisdom and virtue its membership can get on with leading their regular lives of work and family. Indeed Greenpeace has like other global players devoted much attention to developing its brand identity (Szerszynski 1997: 45–6). It has employed

North American symbols, reckless protest actions and skilled use of the media. Szerszynski (1997: 46) notes that Greenpeace's brand identity has 'such an iconic status that it is a world-wide symbol of ecological virtue quite above and beyond the actual practical successes of the organisation'.

So, various networks are developing which are endlessly resistant – forever opposing States and corporations and their 'we-know-best' world which seeks to manage, regulate and order protest. My notion here is that of a cosmopolitan civil society with no originating subject, no agreed-on objects which are to be contested and no progressive Utopias of the future (see Held 1995, Chapter 10, on the notion of democracy as 'transnational'). Globalization, then, can produce a cosmopolitan civil society which begins to free itself from the overarching societies of the contemporary world. It ushers in an immensely heterogeneous and networked civil society, but a civil society which is as much materially constituted as it is social and which may be able to act at very considerable distances, particularly through deploying the global gadgetry of the hyper-modern world. Such a networked civil society will possess significant geographical reach across borders. Intermittently though, its 'members' will come together in the present to 'be with' others in moments of intense fellow-feeling, such as prefigurative Utopias of the present, including festivals, camps or ecowarriors' sites of protest (Szerszynski 1997; see also Friedrich and Boden 1994, more generally on the compulsion to proximity).

The final example is that although clearly one should not exaggerate the degree to which there is globalization of outcome (as opposed to globalization of process), some changes are occurring in what it now means to be a member or a citizen of a given society. I will simplify issues here by conceptualizing citizenship in terms of *risks, rights* and *duties* (see Therborn 1995 for an analogous formulation of citizenship in terms of risk). Citizenship has normally been conceived of in terms of national risks that may face anyone living within a given territory, national rights that anyone should receive and national duties that are appropriate for all citizens of a society. Such notions have of course been implemented in hugely uneven and unfair ways, especially with regard to gender and ethnic divisions. However, underlying such notions has been the prism of *social* governmentality. Rose (1996: 328) characterizes this as: 'Government from "the social point of view"'. He summarizes how in the British context: 'codifiers such as Beveridge and Marshall constructed a vision in which security against hardship, like hardship itself, was social and to be provided by measures of benefit and insurance that, in name at least, were to be termed "universal", including all within a unified "social citizenship"' (p. 345).

Such governmentality was effected through new forms of expertise, partly based upon sociology as the science of such societies. However, Rose goes on to demonstrate that with globalization and the re-emphasis upon the category of the community there is a desocialization of especially economic government – a decoupling of economic strength and social welfare, a contradiction between the social and the economic and a more general collapse of the power of the social akin to much of what I have argued here.

What Rose does not go on to consider are the possible contours of *global* citizenship, its relationship with national citizenship and the role of certain objects and images in potentially producing and sustaining such a global citizenship. Such a citizenship involves global risks, rights and duties, and I take each of these to be constituted in a cultural/material and not strictly legal sense. Global risks include:

- environmental or health 'bads' especially resulting from what is conceptualized as global environmental change;
- cultural homogenization which destroys local cultures (so-called 'coca-colonization');
- the development of diseases which are carried across national borders by travellers (AIDS);
- the collapse of world markets particularly for agricultural commodities;
- financial meltdowns and their devastating effects on particular places;
- the widespread destruction of local economies especially in the developing world;
- the proliferation of hugely insecure and out of control 'wild zones' (such as the former Yugoslavia and Somalia).

Global rights might be thought to include:

- access to the Internet and other electronic forms of communication;
- the ability to migrate from one society to another, to stay and to return;
- the ability to carry one's culture and its central icons with one and to encounter on arrival a hybrid culture containing some elements of one's culture;
- the ability to buy across the globe the products, services and icons of diverse other cultures;
- the ability to form social movements with citizens of other cultures to oppose particular States (e.g. the UK as the 'dirty man of Europe'), sets of States (e.g. the North), corporations (e.g. Shell) and general 'bads';
- the ability to engage in leisure migration throughout almost all the 200 countries of the globe and hence to 'consume' all those other places, objects and environments;
- the ability to inhabit environments which are relatively free of risks to health and safety and to enjoy clean air, water, land and food;
- being provided with the means by which to know about those safe environments through multimedia sources of information, understanding and reflection (see Secrett 1997 on such inalienable environmental rights).

Global duties might be thought to include:

- finding out the state of the globe, both through national sources of information but especially through international sources;
- demonstrating a stance of cosmopolitan openness towards other environments and cultures;
- engaging in appropriate forms of behaviour with regard to other cultures, environments and politics which are consistent with notions of sustainability;

- responding to images, icons, narratives and so on, which address people as citizens of the globe rather than purely as citizens of a nation, ethnic group, gender, class or generation;
- seeking to convince others that they should also seek to act on behalf of the globe as a whole and not of particular bounded territories.

My point in this section is not of course to suggest that the world's population are all citizens of the globe and that a new social – the global – has replaced the old social, the societal. I am not suggesting this partly because such developments are all as yet on a minor scale and for most people in their daily life the 'national' is still of more significance than the global. In addition, global analysis brings out the centrality of *inhuman* objects to the constitution of contemporary networks. Such networks have literally to be made and remade through machines, technologies, objects, texts, images, physical environments and so on. In relation to global citizenship the following objects are constituting the network which may eventually produce such a citizenship: images of the globe and of various threats to the globe; various new electronic media and global media empires; large-scale travel mobility; the development of worldwide credit cards; the movement of waste risks across the globe; the development of global advertising campaigns and techniques; and so on (see Anderson 1989 on the analogous role of print capitalism in relation to the imagined community of the nation; see Ritzer 1995 on the global credit card).

I have argued in this section that in four different contexts, computer networks, consumerism in Eastern Europe, sociational opposition and new modes of citizenship, there are powerful new temporal-spatial networks of the human and the inhuman. These new configurations weaken the power of the societal to draw together its citizens as one, to govern in its unique name, to endow all with national identity and to speak with a single voice.

Conclusions

This discussion has generated many loose ends. Overall I have tried to show that to the extent to which human beings can be said to possess powers, these mainly derive from their complex interconnections over time and across space with material objects, signs, machines, technologies, texts, physical environments, animals, plants and waste products. People appear to possess few powers which are purely human, while most can only be realized because of their connectedness with these inhuman components. This inability of humans to act in some sense or other *on their own* appears to be increasingly marked because of a range of new developments: the miniaturization of electronic technologies into which humans are in various senses instantaneously 'plugged in'; the transformation of biology into genetically coded information; the increasing scale and range across time and space of intensely mobile waste products and viruses; the hugely enhanced capacities to simulate the spaces of nature and culture; and the more general transformation of informational and communicational flows which dramatically compress or de-territorialize distances of time and space between people.

Thus those entities which appear to be of causal importance in the contemporary world are not the product, intended or unintended, of humans acting on their own and realizing their supposedly specific powers. Indeed the role of the human may be exceptionally limited and impossible to identify separately from their interconnections with these other elements. There is then no distinct level of *social* reality, if this implies that there are social entities which are the particular and unique outcome of humans acting in and through their particular powers. In particular, since all apparently social entities in fact involve networks of connections between humans and these other components, then there are no such entities as human societies. If there are no humans any more, so there are no (human) societies. There is, one might say, 'no such thing as society'. None of this however implies that humans are not hugely constrained by powerful forces beyond their control – but these are to be viewed as less purely social or societal and more inhuman or cultural, where culture is seen to embrace what is often known as 'material culture'.

I have also shown that the widespread reference to *globalization* and the *global* in many academic and policy discourses reflects this increased awareness of the power of the inhuman and the limitations of social or societal relations and of discourses focussing upon the social. I have emphasized the importance of analysing global networks in which are combined various human and inhuman components, including informational transfers (global financial trading), human actions (travel), technologies (media/Internet), waste (ozone depletion), machines (jet planes), signs (the blue earth) and so on. These combine together in complex networks which in transforming the contours of time and space also appear to signify the end of any analysis in terms of the purely 'social', if ever of course this was appropriate.

This can be illustrated through the ways in which all of this impacts upon places. In our *Economies of Signs and Space* (1994) Scott Lash and I distinguished between what we called tame zones and wild zones – wild zones being those place like sub-Saharan Africa, south central Los Angeles, Yugoslavia, many European public housing estates and so on (Lash and Urry 1994). However, I would suggest that we can distinguish four very broad kinds of zone which might be said to result from the inhuman processes of time and space I have been describing:

1. Live tame zones: advanced consumer/producer services – what has been called the 'cybergeoisie' – working in smart buildings (700 in New York, none in south central Los Angeles); safe suburbs where people have broadly stable identities and people visit safe enclavic leisure spaces.
2. Live wild zones: cultural capital fraction; inner cities with identity experimentation; less safe leisure spaces; alternative tourism; the cosmopolitan valuation of hybridity.

3. Dead wild zones: most people are excluded from the flows except that of narcotics' areas of the so-called underclass; little leisure travel outside such zones; little sense of a work-leisure distinction.
4. Dead tame zones: excluded from the flows but living in secure environments, as in 'Fortress Los Angeles' or British small towns or the countryside; leisure in safe enclaves, defined spatially or temporally.

Those in the live zones move of course rapidly from place to place along various scapes, over or under the dead zones; other travellers may well have to make out in the dead zones, moving from one to the other and never getting to the live and tame zones except perhaps as an employee. This brief characterization of certain new zones in the contemporary world demonstrates how various forms of mobility, travel, electronic information, media images, signs and so on are generating new inequalities. These can be termed 'inequalities of mobility' as opposed to the social and place-based inequalities of the past. This may be the real importance of the so-called globalization of contemporary social life and its transformations of time and space.

Acknowledgements

This chapter is based on a paper given at the International Conference on Comparative Regional Studies held at Sendai in Japan in 1997. I am very grateful for the comments of Phil Macnaghten and Bron Szerszynski on an earlier draft. Also thanks to Greg Myers and Mark Toogood for more general comments related to the current Economic and Social Research Council (ESRC) project on Global Citizenship and the Environment. I also benefited greatly from attending a conference at the Internationales Forschungscentrum Kulturwissenschaften in Vienna on 'Cultures without Frontiers: Shopping Tourists and Travelling Objects in Post-War Central Europe' in April 1997.

References

Adam, B. (1995) Radiated identities: in pursuit of the temporal complexity of conceptual cultural practices. Conference paper, 'Theory, Culture and Society' conference, Berlin, August.
Albrow, M. (1996) *The Global Age*. Cambridge, Polity Press.
Anderson, B. (1989) *Imagined Communities*. London, Verso.
Appadurai, A. (1990) Disjuncture and difference in the global cultural economy. *Theory, Culture and Society*, 7: 295–310.
Beck, U. (1992) *Risk Society*. London, Sage.
Braun, R., Dessewfly, T., Scheppele, K., Smejkalova, I., Wessely, A. and Zentai, V. (1996) *Culture without Frontiers*. Vienna, Internationales Forschungszentrum Kulturwissenschaten, research grant proposal.

Brunn, S. and Leinbach, R. (eds) (1991) *Collapsing Space and Time: Geographic Aspects of Communications and Information*. London, Harper Collins.

Burgess, J. (1990) The production and consumption of environmental meanings in the mass media: a research agenda for the 1990s. *Transactions of the Institute of British Geographers*, 15: 139–62.

Busch, A. (1997) Globalization: some evidence on approaches and data. Conference paper, 'Globalization: Critical Perspectives' conference, University of Birmingham, March.

Castells, M. (1996) *The Rise of the Network Society*. Oxford, Blackwell.

Castells, M. (1997) *The Power of Identity*. Oxford, Blackwell.

Cemy, P. (1997) Globalization, fragmentation and the governance gap: towards a new mediaevalism in world politics. Paper presented at the 'Globalization Workshop', University of Birmingham Politics Dept, March.

Eade, J. (ed.) (1997) *Living the Global City*. London, Routledge.

Featherstone, M., Lash, S. and Robertson, R. (eds) (1995) *Global Modernities*. London, Sage.

Friedrich, R. and Boden, D. (1994) *NowHer*. Berkeley, CA, University of California Press.

Gilroy, P. (1993) *The Black Atlantic: Modernity and Double Consciousness*. London, Verso.

Haraway, D. (1991) *Simians, Cyborgs, and Women*. London, Free Association Books.

Held, D. (1995) *Democracy and the Global Order*. Cambridge, Polity Press.

Lash, S. (1995) Risk culture. Conference paper, Australian cultural studies conference, Charles Sturt University, New South Wales, December.

Lash, S. and Urry, J. (1994) *Economies of Signs and Space*. London, Sage.

Latour, B. (1987) *Science in Action*. Milton Keynes, Open University Press.

Latour, B. (1993) *We Have Never Been Modern*. Hemel Hempstead, Harvester Wheatsheaf.

Law, J. (1994) *Organizing Modernity*. Oxford, Basil Blackwell.

Michael, M. (1996) *Constructing Identities*. London, Sage.

Murdoch, J. (1995) Actor-networks and the evolution of economic forms: combining description and explanation in theories of regulation, flexible specialisation, and networks. *Environment and Planning A*, 27 (73): 1–57.

Ohmae, K. (1990) *The Borderless World*. London, Collins.

Ritzer, G. (1995) *Expressing America*. London, Pine Forge.

Rose, N. (1996) Refiguring the territory of government. *Economy and Society*, 25: 327–56.

Secrett, C. (1997) It must only get better, the *Guardian*, 7 May.

Strathern, M. (1992) *After Nature*. Cambridge, Cambridge University Press.

Szerszynski, B. (1997) The varieties of ecological piety. *Worldviews: Environment, Culture, Religion*, 1: 37–55.

Taylor, P. (1997) Izations of the world: Americanization, modernization and globalization. Conference paper, 'Globalization', critical perspectives conference, University of Birmingham, March.

Therborn, G. (1995) *European Modernity and Beyond*. London, Sage.

Walby, S. (1996) Women and citizenship: towards a comparative analysis. *University College of Galway Women's Studies Centre Review*, 4: 41–58.

Waters, M. (1985) *Globalization*. London, Routledge.

Wynne, B. (1994) Scientific knowledge and the global environment, in M. Redclift and T. Benton (eds) *Social Theory and the Global Environment*. London, Routledge.

2

Internationalizing British Higher Education: Students and Institutions

Tom Bruch and Alison Barty

The wandering scholar has been with us for a very long time. For centuries students have travelled to other countries to broaden their learning and widen their cultural horizons. In Europe perhaps the most famous is Erasmus of Rotterdam, who studied and taught in England in the sixteenth century and was commemorated in this century by the educational mobility scheme named after him. Throughout the world, the number of students studying in a country other than their own has grown enormously in recent decades. The United Nations Educational, Scientific and Cultural Organization's (UNESCO) statistics (UNESCO 1997) show that there were 1,502,040 foreign students in the top 50 host countries in 1994/5, an increase of some 13 per cent compared to the previous year. In the last 25 years, international student mobility has risen by more than 300 per cent, and some commentators expect a continuing massive increase in the next 25 years (Blight 1995).

Various factors may account for the growing popularity of international study, and the interplay among them can be complex. The process of globalization in commerce and communication inevitably affects educational systems and objectives. In an increasingly interdependent world, where communications networks are expanding rapidly, cultural isolation becomes untenable. International experience and fluency in globally important languages, especially English, are seen as highly desirable or even necessary for survival, in relation to both the career plans of individuals and the ambitions of nations. The easier availability of equipment, expertise, research facilities and infrastructure in other countries is a powerful draw.

Improving economic and political conditions in both sending and host countries have facilitated educational mobility, involving both students and academics. More students can afford the costs of international study, using either private resources or scholarships, and more institutional places are available for them in other countries. The development of educational opportunities in host countries may not keep pace with the resources and expectations of students, who therefore look abroad. The ease and speed of travel have generally improved, making the prospect of international study less daunting than a decade or two ago. Receiving institutions, countries and regions have established scholarship or exchange schemes to encourage mobility, such as the British government's Chevening fellowships and the European Union's (EU) SOCRATES and LEONARDO programmes.

A number of commentators have analysed these global trends and offered detailed explanations as to why students study abroad (see, for example, Cummings 1993; Davis 1996). Whether the flow of international students will continue to grow at the high rate of recent years is a matter of conjecture. The prediction of future numbers on the basis of previous trends is risky in a 'market' that is governed by complex factors. The capacity of host institutions to receive international students, for example, is limited. Jarvis has noted that in Australia 'some universities are now reaching saturation point' (1997). The recent currency fluctuations in South East Asia underscore the volatility of international student mobility. The expectations of students and sponsors that their budgeted funds will cover their needs may no longer be so firm, which could reduce the flow of students from that region. The general view, however, is that the number of international students in the world will continue to increase for some time.

International student numbers in higher education in the United Kingdom

The growth of international student numbers in the United Kingdom (UK) mirrors the global trend. In 1995/6, there were 196,346 international students in publicly funded higher education (HE) institutions in the UK (Higher Education Statistics Agency 1997). This represents an increase of 20 per cent over 1994/5 and an increase of 127 per cent since 1989/90 (see Figure 2.1).

Figure 2.1 International students in the United Kingdom

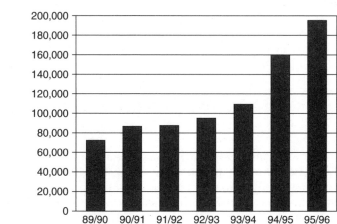

Figure 2.2   Origins of international students in the United Kingdom

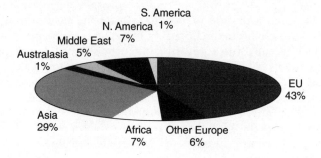

The main sending countries in 1995/6 were (number of students in brackets):

Malaysia (18,532)   Hong Kong (11,283)
Greece (17,053)   USA (8596)
Ireland (16,711)   Portugal (7248)
Germany (12,383)   Singapore (6780)
France (11,296)   Italy (4846)

Students from these countries accounted for nearly 60 per cent of the total number of international students in the UK. Apart from the USA, the top ten sending countries are all in South East Asia or the EU. Nearly 50 per cent of all international students in UK HE in 1995/6 came from European countries (both EU member states and other European countries) (see Figure 2.2).

In 1995/6 international students accounted for 11.4 per cent of the total number of students in publicly funded HE institutions in the UK, and 13.1 per cent of all full-time students. At postgraduate level, international students represented 22.3 per cent of the total and 50.6 per cent of all full-time students. It is clear that international students are a significant constituency in HE in the UK. It is no exaggeration to say that without them, particularly at postgraduate level, the character of many institutions' departments would be transformed and they would struggle to sustain their current levels of educational provision.

Why do international students choose to study in the UK?

The UK is one of the most popular destinations for students from other countries. Education through the medium of the English language is an important consideration for many international students; about one-half of all foreign students choose an English-speaking destination. No doubt the UK benefits significantly from its position as a leading English language country. A student's decision to study in the UK rather than another country, however, is based upon a multiplicity of motives, not merely the language of teaching. The most comprehensive recent research on students' reasons for choosing the UK for study was conducted by the Higher Education Information Serviced Trust (HEIST) in 1994 (HEIST and UCAS 1994). The survey involved 1206 undergraduates from 14 non-EU countries, including Malaysia, Hong Kong, Singapore and others that had a long tradition of sending students to the UK. The survey showed that the most important considerations for students, after the speaking of English, were related to recognition of UK qualifications and the UK's reputation for quality education.

The great majority of international students in the UK are not a captive audience. The percentage of international students that are tied to the UK because they are supported by UK government funding is decreasing. In the expanding global marketplace of HE, where other countries are eager to attract international students to their institutions, the UK will not be able to rely on historic loyalties or the similarity of educational systems in sending countries. In deciding where to study, the students or their sponsoring government or agency will increasingly look to how well the receiving country satisfies their specific requirements – the value of qualifications and the quality of education being the foremost.

Why do UK HE institutions want international students?

UK institutions want international students for two main reasons: they believe that internationalization adds educational and cultural value to the institution, and they want the cash value accruing from full-fee paying international students. An institution is not an homogeneous entity; within an institution, the 'theys' may refer to different personnel and offices, with some holding the first view and others advocating the second. For many both are motivating factors.

There are many staff in UK HE institutions at all levels who believe and argue that internationalization is good in its own right, and institutional mission statements reflect their values. They point to the educational benefits that students and academics from other cultures and systems can bring to the institution, broadening its knowledge base, increasing the breadth and reputation of its research and enriching the curriculum. The presence of international students and academics is also seen to widen the cultural horizons of home students and staff, as well as the wider community, promoting international understanding and, it is hoped, cross-cultural sensitivity. Moreover, the training given to international students by the institution might assist in the development of their societies and even contribute to global political and economic stability.

Alongside these beliefs, institutions are motivated by a powerful instinct – survival. In this society, survival costs money. HE institutions believe that over the last 15 years or so, governments have systematically reduced the vital flow of HE funding to near starvation level. In the early 1980s the UK government encouraged publicly funded institutions to charge higher, 'full cost' fees to international students, and regulations were introduced to allow them to do so without contravening the Race Relations Act 1976. In the context of dwindling central funding, most institutions took up the challenge and began recruiting fee-paying international students, who brought extra fee income to institutions, which they could use as they saw fit. Now, as the 1990s draw to a close, virtually all HE institutions would feel a very firm pinch if the income from international students dried up. Some departments or units, particularly at postgraduate level, would be threatened with closure.

Encouraging international students to come to the UK

As international students are seen by institutions as adding both moral and cash value to the institution, institutions make considerable efforts to attract them. Most HE institutions have international offices that recruit international students through a variety of means: providing stands at UK education exhibitions in the main sending countries; employing local agents to promote the institution; visiting schools, government departments and other institutions in sending countries; advertising in local media; providing promotional information for British Council libraries. In recent years a number of UK institutions have established offshore campuses or collaborative links with institutions in other countries, which both generate extra income themselves and encourage the flow of international students to the UK.

A key organization involved in the overseas marketing of HE in the UK is the Education Counselling Service (ECS) of the British Council. The ECS offers a broad range of services to its subscribers, who include the majority of universities and institutions of HE. The ECS promotes British courses and qualifications, arranges marketing visits, produces market briefings and analyses, organizes exhibitions and missions, and advises prospective students.

Institutions' marketing initiatives in the early 1980s gave rise to a number of criticisms from students, staff and interested bodies. Recruiters were criticized for giving prospective students inadequate information about courses, facilities and procedures. Institutional communication between recruiters and administrative offices or service providers was often poor, at the expense of international students. Some recruitment tactics were regarded as inappropriate. In response to such concerns, a model code of practice for institutions, *Responsible Recruitment,* was produced by UKCOSA: the Council for International Education, in 1987. This was the basis for the British Council's (1995) *Code of Practice for Educational Institutions and Overseas Students,* which makes detailed recommendations related to the expectations of international students, academic matters, marketing activities, information provision, admissions procedures, welfare support and the handling of complaints. ECS subscribers are expected to observe the code and serious violations of the code could result in the suspension of the institution's ECS membership.

Other codes also relate to the needs of international students. The Committee of Vice Chancellors and Principals (CVCP) has made recommendations to institutions that recruit international students in two codes of practice: *The Management of Higher Degrees Undertaken by Overseas Students* (1992) and *International Students in the UK: CVCP Code of Practice* (1995). The then Higher Education Quality Council (HEQC) produced a *Code of Practice for Overseas Collaborative Provision in Higher Education* (1995), which aimed at ensuring that the standards of programmes and awards provided through partnerships with overseas institutions were comparable to those offered by the home institution. The importance of attending to the needs of international students, therefore, has been promulgated throughout HE institutions, including at the most senior level.

None of these codes is prescriptive. In practice most institutions tend to regard them as general guides and implement their recommendations selectively and with varying degrees of seriousness. No external body actively polices an institution's performance in relation to the codes. Violations would normally be reported by concerned or aggrieved individuals, and this rarely happens. The existence of several similar codes may diffuse the attention that institutions devote to them.

In the wake of the Dearing recommendations (National Committee of Inquiry into Higher Education 1997), however, a more formal, structured assessment of institutional provision for international students in HE is being developed. As part of this, the Quality Assurance Agency (QAA) has begun to draft a code concerning student guidance and support, which will also cover international students. It is anticipated that the code will specify what institutions will be expected to demonstrate, and outcomes would be tested when the institution was audited. The QAA is also revising the HEQC code on international collaboration.

The existing codes, though not actively policed, have nevertheless had a positive influence. Most institutions now make genuine efforts to ensure that particular needs of international students are addressed, including providing support services during their period of study in the UK. Such initiatives are not always driven by altruism, however. Institutions recognize that happy students, or 'satisfied customers', will encourage their friends and colleagues back home to look favourably at the institution when considering study in the UK. Whatever the motivation, whether it is centred on the moral or the cash value that international students add to an institution, the demand from institutions for information, advice and training in areas related to international students has markedly increased in recent years. All universities and many other institutions of higher education are now members of UKCOSA, which has produced a wide range of publications, training programmes and other services to meet the needs of institutions engaged in the recruiting and welfare support of international students.

This is not to say that UK HE institutions have been universally and unambiguously successful in meeting the particular needs of their international students. During the last ten years, in general they have tried much harder to support international students, with varying degrees of success. Some, probably a minority, seem mainly to pay lip service to the academic and non-academic needs of international students, providing only basic resources for minimal staff involvement and specific programmes. A few provide imaginative, comprehensive and effective services to international students, systematically improving resources and provision in line with increasing international student numbers in the institution. Most fall somewhere in between. Even within an institution, the quality of provision can vary from department to department. Some institutions rely significantly upon the student union to provide support for international students, and some student unions are excellent at meeting the needs of international students, while others barely pay them any attention at all. Against this background, an international student's experience of UK HE will very much depend upon where and what the student is studying.

The international student's experience of UK HE

Students coming to the UK to study have made an active decision to move out of their familiar environment and to expose themselves to an international experience. In doing so they expose themselves to various aspects of the UK: the academic dimension, the social dimension and the official dimension. The messages they receive from these encounters may vary and apparently contradict one another. While from recruiters and promotional material they may receive the message that the UK welcomes international students into its HE communities, their actual experience before arrival, on arrival or during their stay may undermine these initial encouraging impressions. Students do not necessarily distinguish between the different agencies involved but rather see obstacles anywhere in the system as evidence of a less than welcoming attitude.

The UK admission procedure for HE, through Universities Central Admissions System (UCAS) requires that international students conform to a timetable and system designed for home students. Much of the information requested by UCAS is not necessarily relevant to international students. The UK admissions timetable does not mirror that of other countries: the UCAS December deadline for applications is inappropriate for many international applications and the fact that applications can be accepted beyond the closing date is not made clear to applicants. Applications have to be made through UCAS rather than direct to the institution of choice, imposing delays on applications and decisions which do not apply to procedures elsewhere, for example in the USA or Australia, which as a result may appear more flexible and responsive. UCAS has recently conducted a review of the way in which international applications are processed and recommendations have been presented to the UCAS board. However, accepted recommendations are unlikely to be implemented before the year 2000 entry.

Students may encounter an official obstacle to the UK both when seeking entry clearance and at immigration control on entry. Before being admitted to the UK they have to meet a number of conditions to prove their status as 'genuine' students. This is not unusual, in that all states exercise immigration control and other main receivers of international students such as the USA and member states of the EU impose conditions on students. Nevertheless the delays and attitudes experienced by students in obtaining entry clearance, particularly in certain countries, contribute to an impression that the UK is not wholehearted in its welcome to international students or at least that students from some countries are more welcome than others. It is worth noting that a recent comparative study conducted by (International Development Partnership (IDP) Education in Australia, examining Australia, New Zealand, Canada, the UK and the USA, found that the UK came out least favourably in an international comparison of ease and accessibility of immigration procedures (IDP Education Australia 1997).

Obstacles such as immigration controls inevitably create a barrier to access to HE in the UK. Fees form another significant barrier. The UK charges students from outside the EU a 'full cost' fee. At present this fee amounts to between five and ten times the equivalent home fee that would be paid by a self-financing UK student. According to a further IDP survey the annual costs of study in the UK are higher than those in the other countries surveyed, though IDP and other studies conclude that the UK compares much more favourably when the overall length of courses is taken into account (IDP Education Australia 1997). Fee levels and a reduction in the number of full scholarships available impact on student mobility. Not all students are equally able to meet the cost of HE in the UK. As a result certain countries are better represented than others in the international student population.

Another important consideration for students when deciding whether and where to study abroad, though more difficult to measure, is that of quality: academic quality foremost but also the quality of life in the destination country. International students rate highly the quality of HE on offer in the UK (HEIST and UCAS 1994). However in recent years the rapid expansion of HE together with funding problems has led to anxiety that quality may be undermined. The recruitment of international students has become a priority for institutions as they have sought to increase income from other sources than central government. How far is current interest in internationalization commercially driven and how far does it represent a commitment to an ethos that is not primarily connected with income generation? How far are the arrangements for international students part of a planned strategy for internationalizing the institution and how far are they simply add-on facilities to boost recruitment?

A small, recent survey conducted by UKCOSA (involving ten institutions in the UK, including three new universities, six old universities and one student union, covering England (north and south), Scotland and Wales) asked for information on measures taken to internationalize the curriculum in response to overseas recruitment. Most respondents recognized the importance of such initiatives, though generally the extent to which significant curriculum changes had been realized seemed limited. Initiatives reported include provision of study skills, specific programmes for international students and academic links developed with overseas institutions. There is also a growing interest in flexible programmes of study that allow two years at a partner institution in the student's home country followed by one year in the UK.

Courses, especially in business and management, increasingly incorporate the study of one or more European language and may include the option of an overseas placement, though these activities are essentially European based. Academic links predominately involve students from the overseas partner institution travelling to the UK for part of their programme and staff from the UK partner travelling overseas. It is less common for overseas academics to visit and teach in the UK institution and, despite the desire to encourage mobility among UK students on the part of both institutions and the government, it is less common for UK students to travel abroad to study at the overseas university.

John Belcher argues that all curriculum development should 'incorporate the view that critical thinking is not possible without an international perspective' (Belcher 1995) For many years UK institutions have added an international dimension to the content of some courses, using academic staff who themselves have international experience. Examples abound in development-related fields, but also in courses as diverse as business management and design. Often recruitment for such courses is targeted at students outside the UK and is at postgraduate level. Extending an international dimension into all courses, including undergraduate programmes and those involving mainly domestic students, is rarely achieved. Postgraduate research continues to be more internationally orientated than first degree work (Davies 1994), with established networks of conferences and publications. On the other hand there is growing evidence of the isolation and lack of support felt by some international research students (Okorocha 1997) which profoundly affects their experience as members of their host academic community.

The UK has an established tradition of providing support services for students and still compares favourably with many other receiving countries. As numbers of international students have increased, specialist support services for this group of students have also expanded, often as the responsibility of an international office. Such arrangements offer targeted services which can be attractive when promoting the institution abroad. Discrete services, on the other hand, separate international students from other students and may isolate them (or even generate hostility), when one of the key obstacles to internationalizing the campus is the lack of integration of international students with UK students.

Institutions responding to the survey by UKCOSA were asked to comment on social and welfare initiatives relevant to creating an 'international campus'. Most often quoted were measures taken to diversify catering provision with a variety of meals available to cater to different religious and dietary requirements: for example, vegetarian options, halal meat and varieties of ethnic dishes. Religious needs were also acknowledged to the extent of providing prayer facilities for Muslim students and ensuring that institutional chaplaincies were sensitive to different religious traditions. Accommodation measures included enabling international students to remain in hall over vacation periods, providing some single sex accommodation and mixing different nationalities within flats or corridors. Commonly, institutions organize an induction or orientation course for new international students and may follow it up with other social activities, outings and events – for example a cultural week or an international women's week. The student union may play a significant part in such programmes as well as supporting the establishment of international and national student societies.

As previously stated, international students encounter considerable difficulty in making social contact with UK students while UK students complain that international students cluster together. Much of student social life revolves around the student union where the bars and discos on offer plug into British youth culture and are often uncongenial to international students who may be older, who may observe a prohibition on alcohol or who may prefer to socialize in single sex groups. It is perhaps significant that where many student unions have an International Society, such societies are in practice seen to cater for international students rather than being relevant to all students.

The training available to staff working with international students may usefully increase awareness of students' needs and expectations. However, like other initiatives, such training is generally designed to help staff with the 'problems' of international students rather than to internationalize the services themselves.

It is questionable how deep a contribution these activities, valuable in themselves, make to the internationalization of life on campus. Rather, they largely represent a marginal degree of change leaving the bulk of institutional life unaffected. In fact it could be argued that the environment of some UK institutions of HE is less international and multicultural in character than the environment of the cities in which several such institutions are situated. Overall the experience of both international and British students in the UK is likely to fall short of one which thoroughly integrates an international dimension into the teaching, learning, research, service and administrative functions of their host institution.

Aspiring to internationalization?

What is required by an institution aspiring to internationalization? Aspiring to internationalization is more than increasing the number of international students in order to increase revenue; more than sending academics and marketing staff on missions abroad to sell education to countries where is a potential market, i.e. a gap in the provision of undergraduate, postgraduate or technical education or where British education has a particular cachet; more than adding special services or staff to cater for international students' needs. Where institutions truly aspire to be international, internationalization will need to pervade the institution.

Sven Caspersen, Rector of the University of Aarlborg, speaking at the 1997 conference of the European Association for International Education, described internationalization as influencing the following areas: curriculum, language training, studies/training abroad, teaching in foreign languages, receiving foreign students, employing foreign staff/guest teachers, providing teaching materials in foreign languages, and provision for international Ph.D. students. Changes in these areas go further than developing cultural sensitivity towards visiting students (which, of course, is worthwhile in itself) and affect the nature of programmes available to the whole student body.

Knight (1995) describes an 'activity' approach to internationalization as one which promotes activities such as curriculum, scholar/student exchange and technical cooperation. This is probably still the predominant approach in the UK. Other potential approaches include: a 'competency' approach which emphasizes the development of skills, attitudes and knowledge in students and staff; a 'process' approach which emphasizes an integration of an international dimension into all major functions of the institution; and an 'ethos' or 'organizational' approach, which emphasizes developing an ethos or culture that values and supports intercultural and international perspectives and initiatives. None of these need be mutually exclusive and should ideally support one another.

At present, UK HE risks appearing to put commercial considerations before others. This is certainly often the perception of students paying £6000 to £15,000 per annum. Individual members of staff or departments may be committed to internationalism in its own right but such values are inevitably overshadowed by the prevailing financial climate. Comparison with other countries shows similar concerns. For example in Canada, the USA, Australia and The Netherlands, emphasis is being placed on student and staff mobility, curriculum development, language development, and internationalization of the home student body. International education – that is, internationally *relevant* education – is increasingly being seen as a necessity rather than a luxury: 'High quality education in this day and age is, by definition, international education' (Johnson 1997).

The future of the international classroom in UK HE

When contemplating what the next decades hold in store and how to manage the challenges facing HE, institutions in the UK ignore the international dimension at their peril. Funding issues alone should encourage institutions to focus on their international constituency. There is no reason to believe that any UK government will change the funding arrangements to obviate the need for fee-paying international students. A narrowly revenue driven approach to international students, however, is likely to be self-defeating. Will enough fee payers continue to come to the UK? The number of competitor countries can be expected to grow in the coming years. The USA, Australia and Canada will continue to be attractive destinations, and other countries are also emerging as serious competitors. For example, some regions of China are gearing themselves up to attract more fee-paying international students, drawing students particularly from South East Asia, a main area for recruitment by UK institutions at present.

Moreover, as the HE infrastructure of developing countries improves, the demand for student places in other countries might diminish, or the nature of the demand for international education might change. Instead of encouraging students to travel to the UK or elsewhere, decision makers may place a greater emphasis on creating partnerships with foreign institutions to the mutual benefit of all parties, rather than merely facilitating the flow of income into the UK in exchange for the provision of UK-based education. Although many countries do not currently have easy access to new technologies, technology will undoubtedly be an important factor as well. Why travel abroad if appropriate education can be delivered to your Personal Computer?

As opportunities for home based and international education increase for prospective students, why should they or institutions from other countries still turn to the UK? The UK may find it hard to compete with other countries in providing balmy beaches (global warming notwithstanding), flexibility of study and low-cost courses. The UK has the capacity, however, to offer high quality academic programmes and excellent support systems for international students. Indeed, many institutions can rightly claim to do so. There will always be a market for quality. Institutions that want to be successful in attracting international students and staff in the future, therefore, will need to ensure that they take seriously the quality of their academic and welfare provision. There will be a growing need for institutions to measure their performance against codes of practice and to make appropriate improvements to institutional systems. The new internationalization quality review process (IQRP), which has been developed and piloted under the auspices of the Organization for Economic Cooperation and Development (OECD), will serve as a further incentive for institutions in the UK (and competitor countries) to assess and enhance the quality of the education that they provide in the international context.

Quality concerns will continue to be in the forefront whether the education is provided at campuses in the UK, at offshore campuses of UK institutions, through collaborative links with institutions in other countries, or by distance learning relying on the Internet, video conferencing or other electronic media. The codes and evaluation processes may vary according to the mode of delivery, but the broad issues will be the same.

Crystal-ball gazing is risky, but all signs indicate that internationalization is the future. Peter Scott (1997) has said that 'all education will become international. Our present notion of international education as a sub-component of national education systems, an add-on function, will become redundant'. It is remarkable that the 'Dearing Report' (National Committee of Inquiry into Higher Education 1997) did not address international matters in more detail. HE institutions in the UK will be unprepared for the future if they fail to grasp the need for internationalization.

References

Belcher, J. (1995) Thinking globally, acting locally: strategies for universities. *Journal of International Education*, 6 (3): 7.

Blight, D. (1995) *International Education: Australia's Potential Demand and Supply*. Canberra, IDP Education Australia.

British Council (1995) *Code of Practice for Educational Institutions and Overseas Students*. London, British Council.

Committee of Vice-Chancellors and Principals (1992) *The Management of Higher Degrees Undertaken by Overseas Students*. London, CVCP.

Committee of Vice-Chancellors and Principals (1995) *International Students in the United Kingdom: CVCP Code of Practice*. London, CVCP.

Cummings, W.K. (1993) Global trends in overseas study, *International Investment in Human Capital: Overseas Education for Development*. New York, Institute of International Education.

Davies, J.L. (1994) Developing a Strategy for internationalization in universities. *UKCOSA Journal*, April 1994.

Davis, T.A.M. (ed.) (1996) *Open Doors 1995/96: Report on International Education Exchange*. New York, Institute of International Education.

De Wit, H. (1995) *Strategies for Internationalisation of Higher Education: A Comparative Study of Australia, Canada, Europe and the United States of America*. Amsterdam, European Association for International Education.

HEIST and UCAS (1994) *Higher Education: The International Student Experience*, Leeds, HEIST.

Higher Education Quality Council (1995) *Code of Practice for Overseas Collaborative Provision in Higher Education*. London, HEQC.

Higher Education Statistics Agency (1997) *Students in Higher Education Institutions*. Cheltenham, HESA.

IDP Education Australia (1997) *Comparative Costs of Higher Education Courses for International Students in Australia, New Zealand, the United Kingdom, Canada and the United States*. Canberra, AGPS.

Jarvis, C. (1997) Australia: a new force in international education. *Journal of International Education*, 8 (1).

Johnson, L. (1997) The Internationalisation of Higher Education in the Netherlands. *Journal of International Education*, 8 (1): 22.

Knight, J. (1995) What does internationalisation really mean? *UKCOSA Journal*, January 1995.

National Committee of Inquiry into Higher Education (1997) *Higher Education in the Learning Society: Summary Report* (the 'Dearing Report'). London, HMSO.

Okorocha, E. (1997) *Supervising International Research Students.* London, *Times Higher Education Supplement* and the Society for Research into Higher Education.

Scott, P. (1997) International education on the eve of the election. *Journal of International Education,* 7 (3): 3–4.

UKCOSA: The Council for International Education (1987) *Responsible Recruitment: A Model for a Code of Practice for Institutions Involved in the Education of Students from Overseas.* London, UKCOSA.

UNESCO (1997) *UNESCO Statistical Yearbook.* Paris, UNESCO. (The latest table on tertiary level foreign students can be accessed at UNESCO's web site: http://unescostat.unesco.org/yearbook/ybframe.htm.)

3

Internationalizing British Higher Education: Policy Perspectives

David Elliott (with an afterword by Clive Booth)

In this chapter, 'internationalization' is to be understood as a systematic, sustained effort by government to make higher education (HE) institutions more responsive to the challenges of the 'globalization' of the economy and society. Viewed that way the dearth of utterances on the internationalization of HE as such by the Conservative Party governments in power from 1979 is less significant than the inferences that can be drawn from the fundamental thrust of their general policies, including educational policy, as a whole. This can be summarized as the mobilization of the skilled human resources needed to make the UK a more internationally competitive trading nation, within the European Union (EU) but more especially in the expanding markets of Asia and Latin America. This is linked to a belief in the efficacy of market forces and individualism, a suspicion of social engineering and a principled objection to trade restriction. To the extent that HE has a distinct international purpose within that wider aim, that purpose is to maximize export earnings by selling education services to paying customers. It is unlikely that this position will alter significantly under governments of any political party.

The rationale of the UK's internationalization policy for HE

Legally, British universities are autonomous institutions with varying commitments to international activity in their mission statements. To the extent that their academic communities are able to determine the international agenda, this commitment will be related to their scholarly interests. Few institutions, though, have sufficient non-government resources to operate autonomously. The public funding system, directly or indirectly, conditions whether and how a university operates internationally which, in turn, ensures that 'managerial' as well as purely educational factors shape an institution's engagements. The single most important source of public funds reaches HE institutions (HEIs) via the Higher Education Funding Council, itself derived from government departments, such as the Department of Education and Employment (for England) which, outside of EU obligations, have no remit for international activity.

To the extent that any national body can be said to represent a consensual view of the purposes of HE, this will be the appropriate funding council for the constituent parts of the UK. The Higher Education Funding Council for England (HEFCE), for example, has recently re-stated the purposes of HE as falling under the following headings:

- civilization;
- developing, storing and transmitting knowledge;
- meeting the needs of the economy and industry;
- meeting the aspirations and needs of students;
- serving local and regional communities;
- HE as a tradable activity.

It goes on to say:

> HEIs are now more explicitly concerned with preparing young people for working life, and responding to the needs of industry and commerce. A challenge for the future will be to maintain a balance between this and the less utilitarian purposes of higher education. Important though the economic role is, it is essential that its focus should remain long-term. HE should not simply be regarded as an employment filter, nor is its purpose simply to prepare students for their first job.
>
> (HEFCE 1996: 6)

From our point of view this statement is significant both in what it says and what it does not say. In the first place, the need to insist on HE's non-utilitarian purpose reflects the powerful pressures of the 'market ethic' which British governments since 1979 have vigorously championed, and which the Council itself recognizes when it adds, 'market forces, student choice and the self-interest of individual institutions should continue to be the primary instruments of change'. In the second place, though, the absence of any explicit reference to internationalism, other than 'HE as a tradable activity', reveals more than the limits of the Council's competence (its statutory remit restricts it to the territory of England); it illustrates, at the very least, a reluctance to use the rhetoric of internationalism as it is used by some countries. By comparison there is an absence of diffidence in talking about the need to 'maintain a number of world-class institutions which compare internationally with the best universities in the world'; not least since the Council goes on to point out that in 1994/5 some £200 million was won by them in research contracts from overseas (HEFCE 1996: 6).

From this it can be seen that UK HEIs need to find resources for any non-publicly funded work, including all overseas activity, from other sources.

Many are keen to do so, since universities have always tended to be internationally minded, at least at the level of the researcher. In addition since 1945 there has been a strain of genuine altruism in relation to developing countries. Commonwealth links have provided a focus for assistance to nascent universities, organized first by the IUC, a cooperative company owned by British universities, and subsequently by the British Council. The European ideal itself, as John Davies reminds us, 'provided a strong philosophical stimulus to internationalisation, though the idealism was soon tempered by the realisation that Brussels funds were available, and several universities were predicated on the desire to tap European Community funds' (Davies 1995).

Of British government funds for international activities some is made available, indirectly, by the Foreign and Commonwealth Office (and the British Council) and the Overseas Development Administration. The former provides scholarships and other awards to further national interests by encouraging talented students to study in the UK or assist in the transformation of ex-communist countries, and the latter provides project funding to contribute to the development of Third World countries.

This, though, is probably less significant for many HEIs than non-British government sources of funding including the EU, other international organizations and foreign governments and their citizenry. Here the legal autonomy of British universities is crucial since overseas earnings accrue to them exclusively and are of no concern to the HEFCs. The government encourages HEIs' international enterprises; their overseas earnings make a significant positive contribution to the international balance of payment, while their satisfied foreign clients are likely to be more favourably disposed towards UK interests. For their part HEIs use foreign funds to sustain research and teaching which might be otherwise unaffordable (even if the investment costs in becoming and remaining internationally competitive are sometimes underestimated).

To sum up so far, the relative priorities which the British government, the HEFCs and increasingly the HEIs themselves attach to HE international activity could be represented as shown in Figure 3.1.

Figure 3.1 Rationales for UK internationalization policy

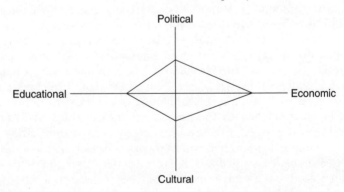

It is worth noting that the relatively low priority given to the promotion of national culture and language overseas by HE institutions is partly because agencies other than HEIs, principally the British Council, exist for this purpose. Besides, it is acknowledged that the attractiveness of British HEIs to international partners and clients is enhanced by their technical expertise being embedded 'for free', as it were, in a pluralistic culture speaking the world's lingua franca.

Policy development

Until the 1960s HE in the UK was almost exclusively the concern of a small number of universities. Compared with those in many other countries they where characterized by social and academic elitism and by a high level of independence from government. The creation of polytechnics (subsequently elevated to university status) and the rapid expansion of the HE sector as a whole from the late 1980s has taken place against a background of reduced public funding per student and a substitution of external accountability for the trust arrangement formerly reposed in the academic collegium. This has led to the emergence of a 'managerialist' style of leadership in HEIs which are, in effect, required to operate as medium to large size businesses. British students, traditionally predisposed to study away from their home towns, have become 'customers' to be competed for; industry has been embraced as a source of contract research; and international opportunities have been vigorously explored by increasingly professional education 'salesmen'.

The increased prevalence of market considerations reflects government conviction that efficiency and effectiveness in any area of activity are directly proportional to the range of customer choice. Organizations will be successful if they are enterprising, i.e. willing to take risks and reward initiative. Therefore in HE as in other areas the role of government 'is limited to creating the conditions in which free competition can thrive. Events and outcomes will be shaped by the market, not by the government' (Scott 1996: 4).

This aversion to social engineering goes back to before 'Thatcherism'. The provision of State schooling in the last century, for example, was a relatively belated and limited incursion into what had been regarded as the proper concern of individuals or their benefactors (and until the 1980s religious instruction was the only subject legally required to feature in the school curriculum). Again many HEIs, before the 1960s, owed their existence to the results of voluntary local initiatives by the business community.

In these circumstances it is not surprising that the 1988 Education Act, for example, was predicated on the assumption that a major role for HE was that it should 'serve the economy more efficiently and have closer links with industry and commerce and promote enterprise' (Education Reform Act 1988). Note that the 1995 Department of Education Review, later subsumed into the National Inquiry into Higher Education (the Dearing

Review) focused on three elements including the role it should 'play in underpinning a modern, competitive economy'. Indeed the merger, in 1995, of the departments (ministries) of employment and education and the transfer of the Office of Science and Technology (including the Research Councils) to the Department of Trade and Industry merely made organizationally explicit what was implicit in the government's ideology.

Perhaps even more revealing of government assumptions about the role of education, including HE, are the three White Papers on 'Competitiveness' which have appeared since 1994 and their 1993 precursor, *Realising Our Potential: A Strategy for Science, Engineering and Technology* (Department of Trade and Industry 1993). The last considered, *inter alia*, how the training of higher level science and technology manpower by the universities could better equip them to fit into the labour market. The context for the 'Competitiveness' Papers is the end of the cold war and the spread of market economies to most parts of the world, which is seen as an historic opportunity for a trading nation like Britain. Trade accounts for 25 per cent of British gross domestic product (GDP), compared, for example, with 10 per cent for the USA, and while the UK represents just 1.1 per cent of global population it is responsible for 5 per cent of world trade. Competitiveness is regarded as being, primarily, dependent upon the skills of the labour force which, accordingly need to be regularly measured against those of our trading rivals and where appropriate improved through setting and meeting national targets. The aim, quite simply, is 'to create the best qualified workforce in Europe' (Department for Education and Employment and Cabinet Office 1996: 21).

There is no comparable government statement on the international role of HEIs as such. While some other governments have produced policy documents expressing their view that HE is an opportunity to 'internationalize' the student population (embracing notions like universal human rights, education for international understanding and peace) the British government has never seen the need. However, the UK has agreed to participate in the aims of EU programmes like SOCRATES which promote a European dimension designed 'to enhance understanding of the cultural, political, economic and social characteristics of other member states' (Davies 1995: 47). (In its response to the Memorandum on Higher Education in 1992 the Department of Education intoned that 'the UK Government's aim is to embed the European dimension in the daily practice of all higher education institutions' without being very specific about the means) (DoE 1996). It is true that greater attention is now being paid to school-level foreign language teaching while, for example, British students comprise 18–19 per cent of all ERASMUS students despite accounting for only 14 per cent of the EU student body (though the UK still imports three students from other EU countries for every two it exports), and British HEIs and research institutions probably receive more than their *strict juste retour* from the EU framework programmes. Nevertheless there is a suspicion of European 'federalism' and of its associated costs (not least the costs incurred as a result of the imbalance of ERASMUS numbers and also by 'free movers': EU students in British HEIs totalled no fewer than 81,000 in 1995/6). Proposals in the 1996 European Commission (EC) Green Paper *Education, Training, Research: The Obstacles To Transnational Mobility* which entail additional expenditure are accordingly unlikely to find favour with the British government.

It is worth recalling that when, in 1980, British policy on overseas students in HE changed by abandoning an essentially *laissez-faire* regime of indiscriminate subsidy (since fee levels were set at levels well below cost), it was intended that EU students as much as those from other parts of the world would be required to meet all the costs of their tuition (a position which was shifted only following legal appeal). Some Commonwealth governments have pointed out ruefully that the savings to the British exchequer made by charging their students have been outstripped by far by the financial burden of being the most attractive destination for non-fee-paying EU students.

The 1980 policy change, actually prompted by the decision of the government to find savings across the board (and so little did the Department of Education consider the international significance of this particular 'saving' that the Foreign Office, apparently, was as surprised as overseas authorities by their volte-face over fees), caused considerable dismay in the academic community at the time. This was both because it affected most adversely students from the poorest countries (in response to which the British government subsequently introduced a package of ameliorating measures) and because HEIs' public funding was cut by the estimated value of the foregone subsidy. This left HEIs with no alternative, in order to avoid making cuts in their programmes, than to replace the lost income, in part by persuading students that a UK degree was worth the (considerable) cost that would now be charged for it. Not until 1984 did the numbers of international students recover to their pre-1980 level, largely by focusing promotional efforts on Pacific Rim countries. By 1995/6 apart from EU students, most of whose fees, like British students', remain notional and whose numbers are subject to regulation by the funding councils, the biggest source of international students was Asia. By comparison with the 56,000 Asians, Africa accounted for only 13,000 – about the same as North America.

Unlike EU students, many of whom study in the UK to improve their English or enjoy a different cultural experience, fee-paying students above all want internationally recognized qualifications. They will have opted for the UK only after making value for money judgements about comparable 'products' in Australia or the USA. Persuading them that the UK represents a 'better deal' and sending them home as unofficial ambassadors of their Alma Maters usually has to take priority over considering how their presence can 'internationalize' the experience of British students. By the same token the large number of EU students at British HEIs – in some institutions probably large enough to constitute a 'critical mass' for 'internationalization' to occur – probably has a more limited impact because their presence can more readily be taken for granted, and they exert little financial pressure on the university authorities. However, this means that on average no less than 11 per cent of the student body at a British HEI is foreign, a much higher proportion than in the USA, Australia or Germany, if the same definition of 'international' is used. Despite this it would not be true to deduce that British HE has been 'internationalized' if that is taken to mean that the curriculum, teaching staff, language of instruction, orientation of research or quality assurance arrangements have been changed specifically to expose the British student population which stays at home to an 'international dimension'.

This begs the question of how to define the criteria by which someone's 'mind set' can be said to be 'internationalized'. If the issue is less the international 'dimension' and rather more 'the contribution of internationalisation to the improvement of the quality of higher education the broader sense' (van der Wende 1996: 59) it is probably true that HEIs' customer focus, which has been encouraged by the pursuit of fee-paying students, has materially benefited UK students; it is also arguable that paying students are more assertive and likely to be a more noticeable presence on British campuses.

Ulrich Teichler, reflecting on the relatively less positive attitudes of British students, compared with other nationalities, to their ERASMUS experiences, has dubbed the UK as an example of 'internationalisation through import' (Teichler 1996). He has written that 'internationalisation requires primarily efforts for the foreign students and scholars . . . [the British] expect that knowledge of the world will be carried to them and will be accessible in their language'. While there is little doubt that some features of cosmopolitanism – such as versatility with foreign languages – remain relatively underdeveloped, it is less clear that this has resulted in British students being less wedded to internationalist desiderata like multiracialism and multiculturalism.

Certainly in at least one respect, because of financial imperatives (rather than internationalism *per se*), the UK has pioneered new forms of quality assured 'virtual' international education, for example, offshore course delivery. Just as in the EU the emphasis in achieving a European dimension has moved from student mobility to curricular modification, and even the 10 per cent target set in the original ERASMUS programme has proved overambitious not least because of cost, so too in the wider world there is a growing trend to engage in overseas study vicariously. Usually the aim is to acquire foreign qualifications through various kinds of distance learning arrangements or, increasingly, by enrolling on in-country programmes which have been franchised, validated or established on branch campuses by overseas institutions whose reputation confers status and academic respectability. While there is no doubt that the principal incentive for a British HEI to enter into such collaborative arrangements is financial, nevertheless because what is being 'sold', ultimately, is its reputation the UK has produced a code of practice to guide HEIs through the complex ways in which this can be safeguarded over what can be considerable geographical distances and even greater cultural ones. Moreover such arrangements are now subject to external audit overseas as well as at home. The guiding principle is that the course delivered overseas should in all essential respects be the equivalent of its home delivered counterpart, taking into account appropriate and legitimate local adaptations, including the language of instruction. In some ways, in other words, providing that curricular 'customization' which introducing the European dimension is likely to entail.

Policy implementation

From the foregoing analysis it should be obvious that there are no major schemes or agencies for the implementation of internationalization as such. Certainly not if one takes Skilbeck and Connell's view that a concept of internationalization is 'impoverished' if it denotes only the self-interested operations of nation states through such devices as bilateral agreements and student recruitment – by implication, activities scarcely deserving mention in the same context as non-nationalistic concerns like the preservation of the cultural and physical environment (Skilbeck and Connell 1996).

However if one allows that self- and other-interest may occasionally coincide then the principal means through which the British government contributes to HE's international agenda is via schemes of targeted scholarships, such as the Chevening Scholarships and the Technical Cooperation Training Awards (though as with all development assistance programmes they are judged by their impact on social, economic and political development, not 'internationalization'; indeed the most recent education policy paper from the British Overseas Development Administration (ODA), taking its cue from the World Bank, reiterates the prior claims of 'basic' over higher education because of the former's better rates of social return). In addition to other Organization for Economic Cooperation and Development (OECD) countries, there are technology transfer programmes to developing or transformational economies in the Third World or the former communist bloc such as the Fund for International Cooperation in Higher Education (FICHE) and the Know-How Fund. In all, the British government contributes about £120 million a year to the support of international students through scholarships – while, incidentally, the 'subsidy' of EU students is calculated at a further £200 million (or the cost of four average-sized universities). And in case an impression has been created that British universities are little more than academic businesses it is worth noting that a recent evaluation of the FICHE showed that in the period 1993–6 the government cash grant of £3 million levered £54 million in foregone charges from UK HEIs (staff freely giving their time and expertise to colleagues at universities in developing countries).

Finally, the British Council, a non-government agency, receives around £130 million per annum to further UK interests overseas by promoting mutually beneficial arrangements between British and foreign collaborators, often academic. Among other activities, usually on a shared-cost basis, this pump-primes 1300 research links every year in Western Europe alone. For example, the Acciones Integradas, in association with Spain, which was started in 1983, is financed by each side contributing around £114 million per annum. A recent survey showed that the research groups supported through the programme have gone on to win at least £54 million (£47 million of which came from EU programmes) in follow-up funding. The research initiated has resulted in over 1000 publications in refereed journals, 35 books, 61 conferences and 6 patents. It has also made in important contribution to Anglo-Spanish relations given that over the years the programme has involved 80 per cent of all British and Spanish universities.

However, the activity for which many know the British Council best, apart from the teaching of English, is its collaboration with education institutions through the Education Counselling Service to promote study in the UK. Some 260 institutions pay the council to organize exhibitions, visit programmes, advertising material and so on in the increasingly keen atmosphere of competition to recruit fee-paying students.

The impact of internationalization on the UK HE system

The most obvious way in which some European countries have signalled their conversion to internationalization (or to facilitate the recruitment of fee-paying students) is by introducing or switching to English medium taught courses in order to accommodate or attract foreign faculty and students unable or unwilling to learn another language than their own or English. This has been most pronounced in The Netherlands but is also happening in countries speaking a major world language, like Germany. Clearly this is not necessary in the case of the UK. It is even arguable that the mastery by British students and scholars of foreign languages would significantly change matters: which language(s) should be learned and how far would they sustain international cooperation (rather than international sales) before recourse was needed to the lingua franca English? Of course many students do learn foreign languages and thousands work as language assistants or lektors; however there is not the imperative to speak another language that is felt by non-English speakers, and without the spur of necessity fluency in a foreign tongue, for the majority, will always be more in the nature of an accomplishment.

Compared to many others, British students have been generously supported by the taxpayer. Not only have tuition fees for most first degree programmes been paid by local government agencies, but most students have qualified for grant support towards their living costs. Where courses have a compulsory period overseas these entitlements have been portable. There is, though, no policy that a target percentage of the student population should study abroad in the same way that some governments, for example the Norwegian, have deliberately engineered through their loans and grant systems. This is partly the result of British degree courses being comparatively short and intensive (and until recently mostly non-modular), making periods of intercalated study more problematic. In addition, except for language students, outside of North America and one or two other Commonwealth countries, there has been the linguistic barrier.

Internationalization's most pronounced impact on UK HE institutions has probably been its engendering of 'professional' education exporters. Virtually all universities have teams dedicated to international promotion, recruitment, contract negotiation, advertising, fund-raising and alumni relations as well as welfare support. While much of this would have developed concomitant with HE's massification and the related requirement for HEIs to diversify their income streams, the conversion of non-EU students into income yielding customers and the proliferation of 'offshore' opportunities has been a powerful additional stimulus.

One area where most British HEIs have not needed to make much adjustment in order to accommodate international students is welfare and accommodation. Because of the tradition that British students study away from their home towns, and because they used to be quite young at the commencement of their studies, UK HEIs have invested in providing comprehensive student services – housing, social and medical. Equally, in a multiracial society, it has been relatively easy to cater for the religious or dietary needs of foreign students.

Conclusion

Recent British public debate about the EU has scarcely fostered a propitious climate for promoting 'Europeanization' while 'internationalization' tends to be equated with the commercial challenge of and response to the economics of globalization. The EC's Study Group on Education and Training report *Accomplishing Europe through Education and Training* (European Commission 1996), which, *inter alia*, calls on member states to consolidate European citizenship by 'modernizing' the history curriculum, sits uneasily alongside the concerns of the chief inspector of schools, that British children are inadequately versed in their national history.

While there is no corpus of government policy on the internationalization of HE as such, the utterances of ministers make clear their recognition of the commercial and diplomatic value of the 'education export industry'. A study commissioned by the UK Committee of Vice-Chancellors and Principals in 1995 estimated that international students' tuition fees and associated expenditure in Britain generated in excess of £1 billion a year in invisible exports and helped sustain between 35–50,000 jobs. Indeed the Department of Trade and Industry calculates that the sum total of *all* kinds of education-related exports comes to no less than £7 billion, which makes it one of the country's most important economic activities. The longer term benefits of educating students among whom may be the future leaders of overseas countries is also appreciated. There are, for example, no fewer than 300,000 British alumni in Malaysia alone.

In conclusion, the fact that the British government has not pronounced on the internationalization, as opposed to the export, of HE certainly reflects political priorities accurately. It also, though, reflects the fact that arguably there is less need for explicit policy when, de facto, HEIs' pursue international agendas by virtue of their autonomy, their language of instruction and their academic as well as financial imperatives. But by the same token it is all the more important that individual HE institutions have a clear view of why and how they intend to fulfil their international missions.

Afterword by Clive Booth

David Elliott's chapter was written before the publication of the Dearing Report in July 1997 (National Committee of Inquiry into Higher Education 1997). Has the Report, and the government's subsequent response published in February 1998 changed the picture presented by David Elliott? It is noteworthy that the index of the Dearing Report has no entries under 'international' and only a very few under 'overseas students'. The references to collaboration are all in the context of the home countries of the UK.

Dearing was understandably preoccupied by funding. Indeed, the committee would probably not have been set up at all had not politicians needed a device to defer the thorny issue of introducing tuition fees until after the 1997 general election. It remains to be seen whether the introduction of tuition fees for full-time home and EU students will affect student flows between Britain and Europe. The Department for Education and Employment continues to see the large net inflow of exchange students as a problem and wrote to universities in March 1998 suggesting that they should take positive steps to reduce the imbalance.

Dearing sought to define the benefits conferred by HE for which a call on public funding is justifiable. Broadly, these are presented in terms of improving the international competitiveness of the UK economy by supplying British and multinational employers with high-level manpower. To the extent to which the Committee took account of HE's international role *per se*, largely it is in terms of the ability to trade educational goods and services successfully in the global market-place. The recognition that UK HE is a major export industry in its own right, that it underpins international economic relations and that it needs to perform and be judged internationally, informs nearly all Dearing's thinking and recommendations. One member of the committee, asked in a seminar about the committee's neglect of the political, cultural and educational rationales for internationalization, made it clear that they had hardly entered into the committee's thinking at all.

Nowhere in the Report is there any recognition that HE institutions can or should act as agents for 'internationalization' as discussed in David Elliott's chapter, though there is keen awareness of the importance of international benchmarking of output standards. As a result, many of the committee's recommendations for increasing funding and enhancing quality will, if properly implemented, strengthen the UK's ability to play an international role since, given the degree of competitiveness from other countries' HE institutions, this is crucially dependent on maintaining the UK's world class teaching and research reputation.

Thus, while there may be relatively little in the Report to cheer internationalists or Euro-enthusiasts, probably no major review of British education before has been as aware of the international context in which its future provision should be planned, albeit a context which is characterized almost wholly in terms of commercial competition.

References

Davies, J.L. (1995) University strategies for internationalisation in different institutional and cultural settings, in P. Bok (ed.) *Policy and Policy Implementation in the Internationalisation of Higher Education.* Amsterdam, European Association for International Education.

Department for Education and Employment and Cabinet Office (1996) *Competitiveness: The Skills Audit.* London, HMSO.

Department of Trade and Industry. Office of Science and Technology (1993) *Realising our Potential: a Strategy for Science, Engineering and Technology.* London, Stationery Office.

European Commission (1996) *Education, Training and Research: the Obstacles to Transnational Mobility* (Green Paper). Brussels, European Commission.

European Commission (1996) *Accomplishing Europe through Education and Training.* Brussels, European Commission.

HEFCE (Higher Education Funding Council for England) (1996) *Submission to the National Committee of Inquiry into Higher Education.* Bristol, HEFCE.

Scott, P. (1996) International education on the eve of the election. *Journal of International Education,* 3–4.

Skilbeck, M. and Connell, H. (1996) International education from the perspective of emergent world regionalism: the academic, scientific and technological dimension in R. Blumenthal, S. Goodwin, A. Smith and U. Teichler (eds) *Academic Mobility in a Changing World.* London and Bristol, PA, Jessica Kingsley.

Teichler, U. (1996) The British involvement in European higher education programmes, Society for Research into Higher Education.

van der Wende, M. (1996) Quality assurance in internationalisation, in U. De Winter *Internationalisation and Quality Assurance: Goals. Strategies and Instruments.* Amsterdam, EAIE.

4

Internationalization in Europe

Hilary Callan

At the heart of any serious discussion of the internationalization of education lies a conundrum. How are we to depict the central notion of 'internationalization' itself: as policy, as process, as a self-evident educational value,
as social change with the emergence of new occupational alignments and
accompanying interest, articulation and rhetoric, or as some combination
or accommodation among these? It is a fact that, in Europe as elsewhere,
resources, programmes, institutions and organizations (including my own)
are mobilized around the concept of internationalization. Yet despite many
attempts to formulate a 'tight' definition the core idea remains conceptually
elusive.[1] In part, this elusiveness can be attributed to national and regional
differences in the routes through which ideas of internationalization have
historically emerged. But even allowing for (and alongside) this, I believe
that, without recognition that it is quite differently constructed and represented within these domains, the idea of internationalization will continue
to evade our conceptual grasp.

The primary purpose of this chapter is to examine European approaches
to the internationalization of higher education (HE). In doing so, I shall
seek also to help resolve the conceptual conundrum by discussing from a
European perspective some of the approaches to, and constructions of,
internationalization in the domains of policy, process, educational value
and social/occupational change. In connection with the last of these, I shall
also suggest that the particular perspective from which I write – that of an
independent, transnational, transinstitutional association of highly diverse
groupings of education professionals with 'internationalization' as the common binding concept and banner – gives a view of the field especially
harmonious with the 'disassembled' reading of internationalization which I
propose to adopt.

The role of the European Union (EU) as actor in the internationalization or Europeanization of HE will not be stressed here, since it is covered
elsewhere in this volume. (For the same reason the United Kingdom (UK),
in several ways a special case, is not discussed.) Nonetheless, it is not possible

to ignore the EU as a driving force. From the outset it must be recognized that the influence of events at European level on national policies of member states – those of the European Economic Area (EEA) and those in the pre-accession stage – cannot be excluded from the discussion. Throughout (roughly) the past decade, since the advent of the ERASMUS scheme, community-level actions and policies have become increasingly influential and have cast a long (but uneven) shadow over educational policy and practice at the levels of the national authority, the institution, the international office or academic department, and even the individual actor. Funding sources and levels for the various programmes, rules of eligibility, application, administration and reporting procedures, and (significantly) the growth of a rhetorical tension between calls for a 'European dimension' and for the internationalization of education in the 'new Europe', have had and are having a deep influence throughout the sector, and will be touched on in what follows.

It is also true nonetheless that some observers note a continuing fragility in the institutional penetration of community or government-inspired commitments to Europeanization/internationalization. A single, Danish, example will illustrate both the perception of fragility, and the 'European' versus 'international' tension:

> The demand or need for such an international component of higher education programmes will certainly grow gradually, but steadily, once the introduction of the SOCRATES programme has seen the inclusion of the entire educational system, from pre-school to tertiary level, in a European collaboration on education. The intention is to reinforce the presence of a European dimension throughout the education systems of Europe.

But:

> . . . The internationalization process has been set in motion at the Danish institutions of higher education, though in many places it rests on a relatively fragile foundation. The majority of institutions have set up administrative staff functions in the form of international offices, and international work has thus had a reasonable anchorage in administrative terms. The running of international operations, however, cannot be confined to a single administrative body. Internationalism is gradually meshing largely with the administration of the institutions, where the necessary international competence is still in the construction phase. . . . [The] academic aspect of internationalization is often initiated and developed by enthusiastic teachers, who often make a great contribution to the field – and one, moreover, that unfortunately still goes unheeded in career terms, although possibilities for rewarding this type of academic activity are now gradually developing in the national salary system. Unless the problem of integrating international academic educational activities into the everyday life of the institution is solved, the process

of internationalising higher education institutions in Denmark will suffer considerably as a result.

(Haarlev 1997)

The point at which these forces and tensions will finally come to rest, if indeed any such point exists, cannot be predicted. At the time of writing, a major discussion issue is the extent to which the European dimension will, or should, become 'embedded' in education at national and institutional levels.

Internationalization as policy

In a recently published book, *National Policies for the Internationalization of Higher Education in Europe* (Kälvemark and van der Wende 1997a), the editors' selection of European countries whose internationalization policies were to be described and compared is highly significant.[2] Those selected are Austria, Denmark, Finland, Germany, Greece, The Netherlands, Sweden, the UK and, collectively, Central and Eastern Europe and Russia. As the editors fully acknowledge, the extent to which generalization is possible on the basis of this sample is not clear. In part, no doubt, the selection of countries was determined by factors such as the availability of authors and membership of the Working Group on Western Europe, part of the Academic Cooperation Association (ACA) under whose auspices the research was conducted. The Western European countries selected also feature well-established 'intermediary organizations' standing in differing relationships with the national authorities, but often having responsibility for policy implementation (although intermediary organizations are also found in other European countries such as Spain). Yet the choice reflects other loadings as well: towards Northern Europe (with the exceptions of Greece and the 'East') and towards those countries where it seemed possible to describe the components of a national policy, however simple or complex this might be. These loadings are scarcely surprising, given the extreme diversity within Europe of educational systems, traditions, national priorities and relations between the HE sector and the State.

At the same time, both the selection of cases for this study, and the differences within the sample, raise the pertinent question 'What is it to have a policy for internationalization?' Among European countries there is enormous variation in the degree of explicitness and cohesion of any national policy on internationalization of HE, and in the linkage (if any) between this and other policy areas and priorities. To restrict discussion and comparison to those countries possessing a declared national policy on internationalization within a political structure which makes this possible, is to exclude large and important parts of the European tapestry. Unfortunately, the information is not available which would make possible a comprehensive analysis; but a few contrasting cases will serve to illustrate the point.

The Netherlands provides a good example of an explicit national policy for internationalization, clearly and transparently tied to policy goals and instruments at national level, and seen as complementary to actions of the EU (see, for example, van Dijk 1997; Johnson 1997). This transparency, rooted in the traditions of the Dutch political process, makes it relatively easy to 'track' shifts in national policy and their impact on institutions and activities. For The Netherlands the past ten years have seen a clear movement away from a generalized policy for the stimulation of international links in HE, driven by educational aims, towards a policy of far more selective interventions based on a view of education as an agent in raising the competitiveness of the Dutch national economy. The history of the STIR programme offers a good illustration of this shift. This programme, originally set up in 1988, was a general stimulation fund designed to give across-the-board funding to institutions for the support of international activity. It ran until 1996 and supported a number of activities, primarily focused on mobility but including also staff exchange, the building of institutional infrastructures and networks, and curriculum development. National priorities changed; and the winding-down of STIR left a significant gap in funding for institutions' international activities. This in turn has been partly met by increased levels of support targeted at highly specific objectives: notably, cooperation with neighbouring countries, export of knowledge (recruitment of fee-paying international students) and, most recently, a programme of support for gifted students for study abroad. Johnson (1997: 31) summarizes the policy shifts of the past few years as follows:

> . . . [g]eneric stimulation of the internationalization process by the Dutch government has come to an end and is being replaced by a more modest programme of selective stimulation. The focus has shifted and internationalization will only be funded on an incidental basis and in line with government economic policy rather than institutional policy . . . Small programmes offering grants to an élite minority of particularly gifted students to enable them to carry out activities in support of longer term national economic aims, and money for institutional cooperation within regions targeted for strategic reasons by the government, have replaced the programmes which allowed the universities to determine, within broad guidelines, how and when mobility grants should be allocated and with which international partners they wished to cooperate.

The case of Sweden presents some interesting similarities and contrasts of emphasis with that of The Netherlands. In Sweden also, the evolution of a highly explicit set of priorities for internationalization has reflected a consciousness of broader national interest. Being, like The Netherlands, a country whose language is less widely spoken and taught, Sweden has a historic concern to establish and maintain its position in global educational, cultural and economic spheres; and, as in other 'minority language' countries, the issue of language in education has been important (see below).

The need for language competence has been consistently emphasized in government policies – backed by funding – for internationalization of campuses and for integration of international components into curricula. Related to the language question is that of the influence of, and links with, the educational traditions of other countries; for Sweden, according to Kälvemark (1997), a historical association with the German academic tradition has in recent years been overtaken by Anglo-Saxon influences.

In terms of student mobility, the effect of national policies over the past few years has been to encourage increasing numbers of Swedish students to spend periods of study abroad, aided by the portability, under certain conditions, of State grants and loans (Kälvemark 1997). Despite the fact that foreign students do not pay tuition fees, inward mobility levels are lower, and (in contrast to recent shifts of policy emphasis in The Netherlands and to the long-standing position of the United Kingdom) the doctrine of HE as an export industry does not seem to be a part of Swedish national policy (Kälvemark 1997).

One feature to emerge strikingly from the Swedish case is the 'internested' quality of national perspectives on internationalization of education. A strong commitment to Nordic regional cooperation, and sense of partnership in what one might call a 'Nordic educational space', coincides with commitments to participation in educational programmes at EU level and with broader global outreach – notably in the transatlantic and 'north-south' directions. Clearly, these parallel commitments reflect the recent history of Sweden's international relations in general, and its accession to the EU in particular.

Two further features of the Swedish case are worth noting here, because they are likely to become increasingly important elsewhere in Europe in the near future. The first of these is the link between HE and the business and commercial sectors. The promotion of this link is, of course, not new in many parts of Europe, where governments have for some years encouraged industry-university partnerships. The Swedish government has however recently taken the further step of enshrining private sector participation in the governance of universities. The impact of this policy move on the international dimension of education, and the possible models it will provide for other European countries, will be intensively debated. The second feature of note is the Swedish commitment to regional and cross-border educational cooperation, reflected in the Nordic grouping and in close and growing associations with the Baltic States and North-Western Russia. This also appears, as we have seen, in the Dutch case, where it is given a somewhat different emphasis. As a general theme, it is attracting growing interest and discussion within Europe. A number of cross-border institutional partnerships and networks are in place, and models are being developed of common interests which can be identified and pursued by cross-border partners on the peripheries of nation-states as an alternative (and perhaps as a political counterweight) to policies emanating from the 'central' level of national governments.

The cases of The Netherlands and Sweden, here cited in a highly compressed and selective way, are excellent examples of countries in Europe where internationalization of education takes place under the influence of explicit, historically layered national goals which are themselves the outcome of well-understood political processes and traditions. What of countries where this does not hold, or does so to a lesser extent? These present, in a sense, more challenging problems for analysis and comparison, since it is necessary to elicit or deduce 'tacit' policies from actual commitments or actions at national level. The question of how far such 'tacit' policies can be validly compared with those which are explicitly stated cannot be addressed here. The problem facing any attempt at comparative analysis across Europe is that – in general and with exceptions – it is in the countries of the north and west of the continent that the explicit and coordinated national policies tend to be clustered. This is not, of course, to say that there is an absence of national policy in countries of Southern Europe; such is far from being the case. It is true, however, that for some of these countries a different approach, and different kinds of evidence, are relevant to the determination of a national policy. Not everywhere is it possible to state national policy in a definitive manner, based on a unified and transparent authority and single policy-making process.

One illustration of the need to take account of relatively indirect indicators of national policy is provided by the existence, in a number of countries, of bilateral or multilateral ties and cultural agreements providing for educational cooperation with other nations or regions. Many 'developed' countries in Europe have these ties, often based on former colonial relationships: an obvious example is the UK's participation in Commonwealth programmes such as CSFP (Commonwealth Scholarship and Fellowship Programme), CUSAC (Commonwealth Universities Study Abroad Consortium) and the Commonwealth of Learning. In parallel manner, and backed by considerable investment of resources and infrastructure, France, Spain and Portugal among European countries have national policy commitments to broadly-based educational cooperation with, respectively, Francophone, Spanish- and Portuguese-speaking partner countries outside Europe with which they have historical and cultural ties. Whether or not these programmes fall administratively within a framework of internationalization of education (sometimes, in fact, they are the responsibility of ministries of foreign affairs or development cooperation, or specialized national agencies) they clearly contribute an international dimension to HE at policy level in the countries concerned.

A second illustration can be found in the selectiveness with which some European countries attach priority to the conventionally recognized components of internationalization such as student and staff mobility, internationalization of curricula, credit recognition and transfer, and research cooperation. A case in point is provided by Greece, which as stated earlier is the only country of Southern Europe to be included in the 1997 ACA study and which has historically, owing to massive under-supply of domestic HE in relation to demand (Callan and Steele 1992) been a large net 'exporter' of students to other parts of Europe and the USA. From the description and figures given by Antoniou (1997) it is clear that all these components, especially ECTS (European Credit Transfer System) have greatly enhanced the international character of the national education system; as have the increased use of English as the language of instruction in some postgraduate courses, and the growth of participation in the EU exchange and mobility programmes. At the same time, it is evident that the focus of national policy is support for mobility. Under the government's programme for scholarship support, awards are targeted both to Greek nationals for study abroad under the EU programmes or at postgraduate level, and also to foreign students and ethnic Greeks for study in Greece. This, then, is an example of national policy which is ostensibly tied to mobility, but in which the 'added value' of increased and balanced mobility to the broader international dimension of education is also fully recognized.

Internationalization as process

The 'process' approach to internationalization is one of four identified by Jane Knight (1997); the others being approaches based on a typology of activities, on the development of competencies, and on the fostering of an international ethos or values on campus. Knight's conceptual distinctions are especially valuable in discussing the varying profiles of internationalization in Europe. Particularly useful is the distinction she draws between policy orientations based on *activity*, and those based on *process*. This difference of orientation is helpful in interpreting the diversity we see on the ground within Europe.

In much of the current literature, discussion of internationalization as process focuses on the institutional level, and stresses institutional transformation as a goal or concomitant of internationalization. Knight (1997) is very clear on the point:

> The concept of integration is key to the process approach. First, there is the integration of the international and/or intercultural perspective into the primary functions of teaching, research and service. Secondly, integration refers to the coordination of the various international activities to ensure that . . . there is a mutually beneficial relationship among initiatives . . . Finally, the international dimension needs to be integrated into the mission statement, policies, planning and quality review systems to ensure that internationalization is central to the institution's goals, programmes, systems and infrastructure.

In a European context, similar thinking can to some extent be applied at the level of national policies and commitments. One way of examining the 'process' dimension of internationalization at national level is to consider the integration of internationalization policies with, and their impact on, the national HE system itself. This question was addressed in the ACA comparative study (Kälvemark and van der Wende 1997a) in the context of the selected sample of countries included in the study. Van der Wende (1997b) finds a general tendency to reduction of the discontinuity between general education policies and those for internationalization, shown for example in the emergence of integrated budgets and inclusion of internationalization into planning cycles and quality-assurance instruments at national level, while also noting areas of continuing disconnection. Kälvemark and van der Wende (1997b) draw the general conclusion that:

> The development towards more comprehensive policies can be considered as positive in the view of sustainable changes in education. Moreover, the initially very narrow definition of internationalization in terms of international academic mobility is now being widened. This contributes to diminishing the conceptual disconnection between internationalization and higher education policy in general. Also in practical terms, the more comprehensive and multi-layer strategies can be expected to create better conditions towards a narrowing of the gap between the two areas of policy-making.

On the basis of the comparative study, these authors thus suggest a developmental connection between integrated national policies, systemic change, and a shift from activity-based to process-based thinking on internationalization. However, in view of the unavoidable limitation and loading of the sample as noted earlier, and the absence of comparable information on countries where policies are tacit rather than declared, it would be premature to claim this as a general principle applying to European education. While in historical terms it is too early in the evolution of international education in Europe to speak with any confidence of a general movement from 'activity-based' to 'process-based' national approaches, it is certainly true that European countries show considerable variation along a conceptual axis with systemic transformation at one extreme, and activity-based commitments at the other.

For the countries eligible to participate in the EU programmes, a complicating factor once again is the tension between 'internationalization' and 'Europeanization'. For participating institutions in these countries, the advent of the SOCRATES programme in particular has brought pressure for institutional transformations designed to encourage the European dimension to become rooted in their philosophy and strategic orientation. As in the Dutch and Swedish cases cited above, it is common for structural responses to the incentives for 'Europeanization' coming from the current generation of EU programmes to coexist with, and be layered upon, broader and often older forms and directions of internationalism. Many institutions and educators see the European dimension as integral to a more broadly-based international outlook, and favour administrative arrangements which reflect this view. On many sides, calls are being heard for a reassertion of the principle of subsidiarity in a manner that would assure autonomy to national authorities and institutions to develop their own balance among international and European imperatives in the content and organization of teaching and learning. Also being called for is a greater degree of flexibility and mutual trust in the relations between the major actors (the European Commission, national authorities, and institutions) in the management of the European-level programmes. These calls, if heeded, could in the future have the effect of fostering a more transparent, creative and stimulative relationship between 'Europeanization' and 'internationalization' as mutually supportive processes. At the time of writing (early 1998) however, the situation is one of flux, with institutions and national authorities in the eligible countries reflecting on one year's experience of the current EU programmes; with more change heralded by the accession of new countries to these programmes; and with intense discussion and consultation taking place throughout the Union on the decisions which will create the next generation of programmes after 1999. Consequently, the future connections between 'Europeanization' and 'internationalization' cannot be easily predicted.

Internationalization as educational value

Under this heading I include policies and commitments having to do with specifically educational goals and the role of internationalization in achieving these. Also included would be perceptions of institutional change and enabling instruments directly serving these goals. Hence it is important here to define and take into account educational value accruing from internationalization to all the actors involved: students and staff (both mobile and non-mobile) and any generalized educational benefit to institutions and the broader community they serve.

Here, however, we run up against a difficulty. There is strong pressure in Europe (some of it coming from policy commitments at EU level) on educators and governments to elide the objectives of excellence in education (including lifelong learning) for its own sake, with those of education for employment and economic prosperity. These, I would suggest, are legitimate and connected goals, but they are not the same goal. Elsewhere (Callan 1998) I have argued the need in a European context for the independent voice of educators to be heard more strongly than at present in pinpointing the specifically educational 'added value' of the exchange and mobility programmes, as a counterweight to programme-driven thinking which, in turn, reflects the wider political and economic (as well as educational) commitments of the EU. In the broader context of this discussion, I would urge the same case: that the educational rationales for internationalization cannot be taken for granted but need to be articulated, lest they be subordinated by default to other agendas, however valid in their own right the latter may be.

How then are questions relating to the educational 'added value' of internationalization being addressed in Europe? Direct reference to specifically educational benefits are surprisingly sparse in current literature, where the focus tends to be on the production of graduates who are able to succeed in international career environments, and who possess a moral outlook conducive to international understanding. It is remarkable that – if we set aside for the moment debates on labour markets and the employability of graduates, vitally important though these are – there is strangely little systematic or radical questioning by educators of the governing assumptions behind the drive for internationalization. How exactly, for example, do students benefit in academic terms from study-abroad opportunities supported by enabling instruments such as credit recognition and transfer? The existence of good answers to such questions is not in doubt; their neglect can presumably be attributed to legitimate policy concerns with education and employment, and perhaps also to the disjunction identified by van der Wende (1997a) and discussed earlier, between national policies for internationalization and for HE in general. Yet it is striking that of the standard rationales for the internationalization of HE identified by a number of authors in Europe and elsewhere – economic, political/diplomatic, social/cultural and academic (see, for example, Knight 1997; Chapter 2 this volume) – it tends to be the last of these for which the least elaborated case is made.[3]

Language

In a multilingual Europe, the issue of language transects all our discussions of internationalization in the spheres of policy, process and educational added-value, and is never far from the surface of debate. Across the region, language questions are related in complex ways to those of internationalization; but the relationship, as might be expected, differs from country to country. The pull of English as an international language and as the second language of the majority of non-native speakers in Europe is a strong distorting factor.

For the UK (and Ireland), language offers a clear advantage in attracting students not only from other parts of Europe wishing to be taught in English, but from other parts of the world where English is historically entrenched. For other world languages of Europe such as French, German, Italian and Spanish, and for less widely spoken languages such as Dutch, Danish and Swedish as noted earlier, the picture is less clear-cut. In the case of the latter group, the pressure has been on for some years to offer courses in English to international students in order to attract these students as a means of internationalizing campuses and to provide reciprocal study abroad opportunities for domestic students. This pressure has sometimes, in turn, met resistance from domestic students and staff who perceive a risk of 'ghettoization' of international students in English-taught programmes, and/ or are reluctant to teach or study in a language not their own. The policy of the EU has been, and is, to encourage (and fund) the teaching and learning of less-spoken languages in HE throughout the Union. Judging by the powerful lobbying that has taken place during 1997–8 for multilingual competence to be protected and promoted in the coming generation of EU programmes, this policy has the strong support of the international educational community in Europe. Alongside this (and consistent with it) voices are being heard urging that, for countries whose languages are less widely spoken, an effective way to offer incoming students a good intercultural experience – as well as promote a wider knowledge of the host country's language and culture – is to teach courses partly or fully in a majority language, while providing every facility and encouragement to international students for language learning and cultural exposure during their study period.

The sociology of internationalization: a 'professional's eye' view

The last of the perspectives towards internationalization which I wish to adopt in this chapter is that of shifts in the organization of persons and mobilization of interests: essentially a sociological perspective. Alongside the transformations which have occurred in Europe in the spheres of policy, process, activity and (to a lesser extent) the articulation of educational value, the last decade has seen the rapid emergence of occupational specializations and professional groupings. Partly responding to, and partly in turn stimulating the movements to internationalization that have been taking place at European, national and institutional levels, these new professional alignments have had and are having a profound influence. It is not an exaggeration to say that international education in Europe is in large measure being defined and developed operationally, through the work and influence of specialist professionals such as international relations officers, European programme managers, international credential evaluators, research and industrial liaison officers, study abroad and foreign student advisers, and language experts. No theory of internationalization can be complete if the growth and influence of practitioner constituencies is omitted. These constituencies can be examined with many of the conceptual tools familiar to the historian or sociologist of professions, and patterns can be detected comparable to those followed by older and longer established professional groups: the drive for legitimacy and recognition of expertise, entry qualifications, professional development and career structures, instruments of advocacy, networking and professional support.

This professionalization of international education is not, of course, restricted to Europe. Similar processes are well established elsewhere, notably in North America. What does appear unique to Europe is that, partly because of the history and pressures of European integration, ideas of internationalization have had to be forged and negotiated in an environment of massive diversity of educational cultures, economic situations, national priorities and professional interests. My own organization, the European

Association for International Education, can be seen as a test-bed in the interplay of these forces and tensions. Founded in 1989 in order to create a common voice and platform for articulation of the interests of a new professional constituency, its rapid growth and the large attendance at its annual conference testify to the need for a common point of attachment in Europe for the professional aspirations of those working in international education, cutting across the diversity which separates them. Here, the concept of 'internationalization', in addition to its other meanings, functions symbolically as a banner of unity, a rhetorical device making it possible for very different occupational groups to come together as a self-aware constituency, able to define and pursue their common interests. I would also argue, as stated earlier, that a viewpoint from within such an organization places the observer in a good position to disassemble the idea of internationalization and to 'track' the various ways in which it is understood and purposes to which it is harnessed.

Conclusions and challenges for the future

For many years, both in Europe and elsewhere, discussions of internationalization in HE have tended to be dominated by issues of student mobility. This is still to some extent the case, particularly in countries where (and there can be very different reasons for this) mobility is the driving factor in national and institutional policies. At EU level, also, while the old ERASMUS programme has now been absorbed into SOCRATES which combines mobility with other instruments for achieving a European dimension, the view is emerging clearly in current debates on the future of the programmes that mobility, particularly of students, must be protected and enhanced. This notwithstanding, a clear recognition has come about in recent years that to think of internationalization solely in terms of mobility is to take a very limited view. Curricular reform, research cooperation, discipline-based networks and associations, open and distance learning across frontiers, regional and cross-border institutional partnerships, international work placements, and other activities not in themselves new are steadily coming to be perceived as pillars of internationalization, as are instruments of mobility such as international credit recognition and transfer and the promotion of multi-lingualism. This growth of a many-stranded view of internationalization, supported both by national commitments and by enabling instruments of the EU, is one of the most significant current developments in internationalization of HE in Europe.

This is the consensus view to be found in most current writing, and in substance it is probably correct. However, the generalization that can be most confidently made about internationalization of education in Europe is that few generalizations are possible. It would be a massive research task, not feasible within the scope of this chapter or book, to analyse the policy orientations and influencing factors in those parts of Europe where 'policy' is tacit rather than overt, such as countries not included in the sample on which the ACA study was based, to determine whether there are indeed universal directions in the evolution of international education. In default of this, one can speculate and identify issues likely to be, or become, focal over the coming years. My list of such issues would include:

- The need for universities and governments to find ways of 'carrying the torch' of international commitment in face of diminished funding and competing priorities.
- Factors favouring and hindering the institutional entrenchment of international activity and commitments.
- The growth of regional and cross-border alignments.
- The continuing tensions between Eurocentric ('fortress Europe') and outward-looking commitments.
- The growth of links between international education and international business and commerce, and their implications.
- The need to articulate a strong set of specifically educational and intellectual rationales for internationalization.

One of the problems in discussion of internationalization of education is the very power and success of the idea, both substantively and rhetorically. As others have rightly said, we face a future in which all education will be international. How will it be possible to map this future, and to make judgments about directions and priorities? In this chapter I have tried to indicate a disassembled approach to internationalization which would enable the idea's many layers and constructions to come into view and be addressed. Whether or not this suggestion is taken up in research, it seems clear that statements of faith in an international future will not be enough to see us through.

Notes

1. Knight (1997: 42) offers an institution-based 'working definition' of internationalization as follows: 'Internationalization of higher education is the process of integrating an international/intercultural dimension into the teaching, research and service functions of the institution'.
2. This excellent book, on which I have drawn extensively for this chapter, provides an up-to-date comparative analysis of national policies in selected European countries at a level of detail which cannot be covered here. It is highly recommended for further reading.
3. Knight, presenting a general theoretical introduction to country studies outside Europe, writes of tensions between a belief in internationalization as a factor in formulating and achieving 'international standards' in teaching and research, and concerns over the possible 'homogenization' of scholarship. Tellingly, she writes that:

> It can be rigorously debated whether internationalization is an end in itself, as is often articulated, or a means to an end, with the end being the

improvement of the quality of education. It is assumed that by enhancing the international dimension of teaching, research and service there is value added to the quality of our higher education systems. This premise is clearly based on the assumption that internationalization is considered to be central to the mission of the institution and is not a marginalised endeavour.

(Knight 1997)

She goes on to suggest that the 'added value' of internationalization to the educational process may come about indirectly, through its positive influence on institution-building.

References

Antoniou, A. (1997) Greece, in T. Kälvemark and M. van der Wende (eds) *National Policies for the Internationalization of Higher Education in Europe.* Stockholm, National Agency for Higher Education. Högskoleverket Studies 1997: 8.

Callan, H. (1998) Future focus: the European dimension and beyond. *Journal of International Education*, Spring.

Callan, H. and Steele, K. (1992) *Student Flow and National Policy in the EC.* London, UKCOSA and Commonwealth Secretariat.

Haarlev, V. (1997) Denmark: general outline of the Danish national policy for internationalization of higher education, in T. Kälvemark and M. van der Wende (eds) *National Policies for the Internationalization of Higher Education in Europe.* Stockholm, National Agency for Higher Education. Högskoleverket Studies 1997: 8.

Johnson, L. (1997) The internationalization of higher education in The Netherlands. *Journal of International Education*, 8 (1): 28–35.

Kälvemark, T. (1997) Sweden, in T. Kälvemark and M. van der Wende (eds) *National Policies for the Internationalization of Higher Education in Europe.* Stockholm, National Agency for Higher Education. Högskoleverket Studies 1997: 8.

Kälvemark, T. and van der Wende, M. (eds) (1997a) *National Policies for the Internationalization of Higher Education in Europe.* Stockholm, National Agency for Higher Education. Högskoleverket Studies 1997: 8.

Kälvemark, T. and van der Wende, M. (1997b) Conclusions and discussion, in T. Kälvemark and M. van der Wende (eds) *National Policies for the Internationalization of Higher Education in Europe.* Stockholm, National Agency for Higher Education. Högskoleverket Studies 1997: 8.

Knight, J. (1997) Internationalization of higher education: a conceptual framework, in J. Knight and H. de Wit (eds) *Internationalization of Higher Education in Asia Pacific countries.* Amsterdam, European Association for International Education.

van der Wende, M. (1997a) Missing links, in T. Kälvemark and M. van der Wende (eds) *National Policies for the Internationalization of Higher Education in Europe.* Stockholm, National Agency for Higher Education. Högskoleverket Studies 1997: 8.

van der Wende, M. (1997b) International comparative analysis and synthesis, in T. Kälvemark and M. van der Wende (eds) *National Policies for the Internationalization of Higher Education in Europe.* Stockholm, National Agency for Higher Education. Högskoleverket Studies 1997: 8.

van Dijk, H. (1997) The Netherlands, in T. Kälvemark and M. van der Wende (eds) *National Policies for the Internationalization of Higher Education in Europe.* Stockholm, National Agency for Higher Education. Högskoleverket Studies 1997: 8.

5

Internationalization in South Africa

Roshen Kishun

At last we have joined the march with the rest of the world where our destiny is in our own hands.

(Thabo Mbeki 1996)

The globalization of education in South Africa cannot be seen in isolation to the momentous developments that have taken place in the last 5 years, and for that matter, to the history of the region in the last 500 years. While the legacy of the imported educational systems from the colonial powers still prevails, the rapid reintegration into the world community after the 1994 election of a democratic government in South Africa presented challenges and opportunities for fundamental transformation of the society in general and higher education (HE) in particular.

The HE sector was impacted by some of the most powerful forces of globalization including the domination of the 'market ideology', the process of massification, the technology revolution, and the emergence of a socially distributed knowledge production system. All these trends are expected to have a profound influence on the manner in which a democratic country achieves its goal of reconstruction and development while aiming to be a global player in the new world order. Whether we have 'our destiny in our own hands' will depend on how we manage the forces of globalization to meet the basic needs of the country.

While the powerful social and economic forces propelled South Africa headlong into a world that was eager to embrace a democratic new 'African country', the simultaneous response to the global changes and the political transformation in the country led to the opportunity and the imperative to frame macroeconomic policy goals which provide both for increased global competitiveness and for meeting basic needs. As South Africa's long-range strategic objective is to transform fundamentally the education system and to play a leading role in Africa and the wider world, a unique opportunity exists to use international competence, expertise and the technological revolution in a responsible way to achieve the changes outlined in the Government's National Commission on Higher Education report (NCHE 1996).

South African researchers are only beginning to examine the global trends and their expected impact on HE transformation (see Cloete *et al.* 1997; Orr 1997; Subotzky 1997). This chapter is not an analytical discourse or a theoretical presentation around the concept of globalization or the trends and events that are likely to impact the HE sector in South Africa. The primary purpose is to identify some trends and events; to raise critical questions and concerns that need to be examined; to suggest possible areas for research; and to recommend that all stakeholders need to actively examine the structures, processes and policies to maximize and manage the opportunities while not being consumed by the relentless push of the global forces for control and profit.

Reintegration into the world community

A brief examination is necessary of the confluence of some of the factors that enabled South Africa's rapid pace of reintegration into the world community and which are highlighted below. The two developments of great significance for the global reintegration are the membership of influential international organizations and South Africa's role in two regional bodies.

A short time after the 1994 elections South Africa was welcomed back as a member of the United Nations, the Organization of African Unity, the Commonwealth, the International Olympic Committee, the Federation of International Football Associations, the Lome Convention and a host of other international organizations. South Africa's aggressive foreign policy to normalize relationships with countries around the world led to the development of bi-national commissions being signed with the United States and Germany. The more recent diplomatic alliance with China, regarded as an emerging superpower, is significant as China's impact 'on the world in the twenty-first century could be even more than that of the United States in this century' (Naidoo 1998).

South Africa is playing a leading role in the Indian Ocean Rim Association for Regional Cooperation (IORARC) which consists of Australia, Mozambique, Tanzania, India, Indonesia, Kenya, Madagascar, Malaysia, Mauritius, Oman, Singapore, Sri Lanka, Yemen and South Africa. The Association facilitates and promotes economic cooperation, bringing together representatives of government, business and academia. The University of Natal was elected to be the focal point for academia in South Africa.

South Africa is a signatory to the SADC Human Resources Development Sector Protocol in Education and Training which includes the following 14 countries: Angola, Botswana, Lesotho, Malawi, Mauritius, Mozambique, Namibia, Republic of Congo, Seychelles, South Africa, Swaziland, Tanzania,

Zambia, and Zimbabwe (SADC Human Resources Development Sector 1997). The impact of the agreement has yet to be examined on the HE sector in South Africa.

As the world opened up, South Africans of course discovered that it had catching up to do in science and technology, arts and culture, trade and commerce, sports and recreation, and governance and management. The years of cultural and academic boycotts have left international gaps in knowledge, information exchange and constructive collaboration that will take some time to fill (Ndebele 1997). On the other hand South Africa has a fairly well-developed tertiary education infrastructure consisting of 21 universities, 15 technikons and numerous technical and teacher training colleges.

Globalization and the transformation of HE

The major thrust of the transformation process in the new South Africa was to create a policy framework within which the educational system would be transformed in the context of the unprecedented national and global opportunities and challenges. The duality of the educational system, the fact that universities no longer have monopoly over teaching, learning and research, and the need for South African institutions of HE to be less reliant on government funds were added factors for consideration.

The fundamental questions that we needed to ask as a nation that was suddenly thrust upon the world went to the heart of who we represented and how we wished to provide the leadership required (Ndebele 1997: 3). What are our framing values and how do we promote them? What aspects of our tertiary education do we need to promote? What are the opportunities and limits of globalization? What is the role of foreign expertise in our democracy? What are the curriculum implications of multiculturalism and internationalism? What do these curriculum questions mean for individual cultures, and how do these cultures define the entire tertiary education system and the production of knowledge? To what extent do we open our undergraduate and postgraduate programmes to international students? What further issues and questions should be confronted to enable us to take a position?

In response to the needs for educational transformation the government, private sector and academia were invited to be the major stakeholders in the development of the 1996 National Commission of Higher Education (NCHE) report, initiated by the minister of education. The report introduced some radical concepts and changes required in a transformed educational system. The report and the subsequent Green Paper on HE transformation (Department of Education 1996) demonstrate a broad commitment to directing HE towards serving both South Africa's entry into the global economy and the basic needs of the majority of the population. However, the more recent government White Paper on HE (Ministry of Education

1997) 'marginalises many of the these issues and focuses unequivocally on globalization articulating the challenges, vision and principles of education. This represents an alarming tilt to the right and uncritical acceptance of the globalization agenda and the sidelining of the concerns of the RDP [the government's Reconstruction and Development programme]' (Subotzky 1997).

The inaugural conference of the International Education Association of South Africa (IEASA) in January 1997 at the University of the Western Cape was an attempt at the national level to identify the trends and events that were impacting the HE sector and to support institutions in developing strategies to manage the internationalization process. The domination of the 'market ideology', massification, the technological revolution, and the emergence of a socially distributed knowledge production system were identified as some of the more important trends that were likely to have major implications for HE in South Africa. While it is a daunting task to predict the cross-impact implications of these trends on the transformation agenda it is nevertheless necessary for HE planners to understand them.

'Market ideology' and 'market university'

Haque (1997: 2) in an unpublished paper titled 'Globalization of market ideology and its impact on Third World development', presents a critical analysis of an emerging pro-market framework that has adverse implications for various groups and classes in Third World countries. He argues that the contemporary pro-market policies are largely based on ideological rather than rational criteria, that the ideological tendencies inherent in these policies can be generalized as a 'market ideology', and that such a market ideology has been extensively globalized in recent years through various forms of influence and manipulation by its national and international advocates. The forces of privatization, deregulation and liberalization have led to the return of 'experts' and 'advisers' to Third World countries. For example, foreign advisers have been directly involved in the formation of educational policy in South Africa. The critical concerns about the differences have been raised relating to both the substantive departure from the NCHE and Green Paper and in relation to the political process by which the White Paper was written (Subotzky 1997: 109).

The 'market ideology' influences the nature of the university towards what has been termed the 'market university'. The primary characteristic of the 'market university' is the commodification of knowledge which can be manufactured, bought and sold (for details see Orr 1997: 46). Market forces are also at play in countries where undergraduate and postgraduate programmes could not function without international students. In these cases students themselves have become commodities in the survival strategies of these universities (Gibbons 1997).

Massification

Globalization has had a profound impact on HE, leading to what Peter
Scott has described as a shift from a 'closed' to an 'open' system (Scott
1995). This 'open' system, accompanied by the egalitarian pressures to
reduce inequalities (Kraak 1997: 62) and the need to promote lifelong
learning are further trends supporting massification worldwide. The White
Paper on Education and Training (Department of Education 1995), among
other recommendations, spelt out the new educational vision stressing lifelong education and training and opening access to those who were excluded
in the past.

The predominant massification pressures in South Africa will come from
two main sources. First, from the projected headcount estimates, the standard ten (school leaving) passes will more than double from 310,000 in 1995
to 640,000 in 2005 (NCHE 1996: 63). Second, demands will be made on the
South African HE sector by the countries in SADC. While South Africa has
21 universities, most of our neighbours have one each. As a result of the
massification in these countries a large number of their students graduating
from high school will seek places in South Africa. The Education and Training Protocol agreement to treat the SADC students as 'home students'
requires that South African institutions examine whether the regional
demands for places can be met or are in conflict with local needs.

The technological revolution

A major investigation in South Africa into technology-enhanced learning
has had to confront the question 'How can the rapidly developing information and communications technologies assist South Africa in achieving the
aims of access, equity, redress and quality in education and training?' (Department of Education 1996). The goal in using technology is to increase
access and flexibility while reducing cost and enhancing quality. According
to John Daniel, vice-chancellor of the Open University in the UK, the proper
use of technology is key to that goal because 'only technology can break the
historic but insidious tradition that links educational quality to exclusivity
of access and generosity of resources' (Daniel 1997: 1). The substantial
increases in the power of telecommunications and information processing
can be used to penetrate all countries, cultures, communication flows and
financial networks for new opportunities of profit making (Castells 1998: 34).

In the South African context two developments made possible by the
technological revolution are highlighted. First, the virtual university concept is a reality and has important implications for HE and the international dimension. The launch of the African Virtual University (AVU) in
1997 with the support of the World Bank, with 17 African countries as
partners (South Africa is not one of them) has important implications for
South Africa. The AVU presents an opportunity for the rapid development

of cost effective resource-based learning, a goal which the South African government and universities have expressed. But the greater danger may lie in the AVU's potential for accelerating the growing intellectual hegemony of the United States and Europe through domination of the content of information and communications technology on which the AVU is based. This could be a threat to the future of high quality, responsive and accessible HE in South Africa as outlined in the NCHE report.

The second related development made possible by the technology that is likely to revolutionize tertiary education is the virtual classroom that will allow South Africans to earn a degree from a university almost anywhere in the world without leaving their home. In the United States there are now more than 1 million students plugged into virtual university lecture rooms compared with 13 million attending actual universities. It is estimated that the number of 'cyber students' will be 3 million by 2000, a growth significantly higher than that for student bodies at the physical universities. 'It is only a matter of time before cyber-learning spreads to schools where students in remote areas plugging into the Internet by satellite and listening to and watching the world's best teachers explaining the world's best learning materials to them' (Mulholland 1997).

A socially distributed knowledge production system

According to Gibbons, many discussions of internationalization leave out one of the most profound aspects of transformation that is occurring internationally – that is, the emergence of a socially distributed knowledge production system (Gibbons 1997: 2). Gibbons refers to the fact that research and knowledge production is now carried out in organizations of many different types. It is not the intention in this chapter to describe in detail the principal characteristics of a socially distributed knowledge production system or to examine in detail the implications for HE institutions. However, the characteristic dynamics of a socially distributed knowledge production that is linked to problem context rather than to disciplinary structures or the dictates of a national science policy, are being adopted by universities in South Africa.

Globalization versus internationalization

'There is no simple, unique, or all-encompassing definition of internationalization of the university. It is a multitude of activities aimed at providing an educational experience with an environment that truly integrates a global perspective' (Knight and de Wet 1997). Many would argue that HE by its very nature is international in character: 'Institutions seek to establish and maintain an environment which facilitates discovery and advancement of knowledge. Such an environment develops and thrives best by exchange and collaboration among scholars with experiences and perspectives from around the world' (Armstrong and Green in Gourley 1997). However, in an environment where the globalization of the economy is transforming HE and is expected to be the driving force that determines the international nature of the university, educators need to examine the forces of globalization, over which there is not much choice versus those of internationalization where deliberate decisions are made regarding what is in the interest of the institution. The distinction between globalization that places emphasis on homogeneity and internationalization that places emphasis on diversity, becomes critical in developing and sustaining collaborative programmes of mutual benefit with international partners.

In the apartheid era the historically advantaged institutions and the historically disadvantaged institutions mirrored the inequities of society. The glaring disparities in the range of fields, low research output, under-qualified academic staff, lack of institutional capacity and infrastructure and the discriminatory way in which funding was provided for the universities have a direct bearing on the impact of globalization. While some institutions were 'fundamentally disadvantaged in relation to meeting the demands of the "market" university and the challenges of globalization' Subotzky (1997: 122) argues that these institutions, through their location and community-oriented programmes, could become important role players in Mode 2 knowledge production that relates to social rather than commercial relevance. This could be achieved through the collaborative partnerships with other regional, national and international institutions (Subotzky 1997). These institutions could deliberately focus their attention on the needs of the country without compromising their research and teaching capacities.

Components of the international dimension

When we speak of adding the international dimension to our education, or internationalizing education, we usually focus on individuals (students) in various programmes or individual academic links. A number of elements or strategies are part of the process of integrating the international dimension into the teaching, learning, research and service functions of HE. According to Knight, the choice of which elements are most important to the internationalization process is determined by the goals, rationale, resources and experiences of the individual institutions, which in turn are influenced by the different stakeholder groups (Knight 1997: 32).

International students at South African universities

In the South African context the most obvious component of the international dimension is represented by international students. In the 1960s and 1970s the Third World was seen as the main battlefield of international academic cooperation and exchange by the world's superpowers. This resulted in a one-way relationship, with student flows from south to north, faculty and funds from north to south. As the global context changed in the late 1980s the economic and political arguments became greater justification for internationalization. South African universities, which are currently facing financial crises, are actively attracting fee-paying international students.

While the major flow of international students are from the less developed to the more developed countries (Wagner and Schnitzer 1991), South Africa has been ranked in the top 40 of the world's host countries. In 1992 only Egypt hosted more foreign students in Africa, according to a report by the United Nations Educational, Scientific and Culture Organization (UNESCO 1992: 3–411). After the 1994 elections, interest from the international community grew and there was a noticeable increase in the numbers of students wishing to study in South Africa. At the University of Natal the student numbers grew by 18 per cent from 1995 to 1996 and by 25 per cent from 1996 to 1997. However, while 'sending' institutions around the world target South African institutions for the placement of their students 'in Africa' few South African students get the opportunity to study abroad. This may be attributed to unfavourable exchange rates, lack of scholarship and financial support, and more importantly to the lack of institutional commitment to encourage students to participate in international programmes.

Curriculum

The internationalization of curricula is one of the most important parameters in the process of internationalizing an institution. Curriculum development is also one of the most contentious areas in an African country where the imperatives of the forces of globalization are part of the package of the economic support and advice from external agencies and consultants. In a market-place where commodities and ideas are strong there may be a danger that the universalizing influence of globalization may destroy the local culture and, local patterns of life, and counteract and undercut the national discourses of citizenship needed to nurture democracy and the culture of human rights (Ekong and Cloete 1997: 8).

The major thrust of the NCHE report (1996) focused on issues of structure and goals, access or participation, governance and funding and the management of the transformation strategy itself. Little attention was given to the content and process of learning. The curriculum transformation was the responsibility of the National Qualifications Framework (NQF) which was established by the South African Qualifications Act of 1995 (*Government Gazette* 1995).

The NQF, described as the heart of the transformational changes in HE in South Africa, helps to explain what the nation wants from learning. The most important qualities are expressed in 'critical outcomes' that would require that educational objectives such as the development of analytical and critical thinking, creativity and problem-solving skills be taught to all students. Because the NQF allows for the development of a new curriculum framework for all general and further education training in South Africa it presents educators and policy makers with the opportunity to examine critically the 'critical outcome' in the global context.

The reasons why considerable interest is given to the international/ intercultural content is that curriculum is core to the education experience and has the greatest potential of reaching the largest number of students (Knight 1997: 33). Promoting the vision of the African Renaissance requires that a way be found of casting the question of curriculum development and change in a framework that nurtures the democratic ideals of an African country while stimulating the expertise needed to compete in the global context. How we do this will depend on the national leadership and the ability of the HE sector to maximize the benefits of internationalization while being sensitive to local cultures and needs.

National policy framework

The internationalization of HE in South Africa has reached such proportions in the last few years that individual institutions have defined, or are in the process of doing so, their goals and priorities in their overall institutional strategic plans. Any university that is serious about the international dimension needs to put in place structures to ensure that there is support to maximize the benefits of having international students, internationalizing the curriculum, etc.

At the national level the government ministries of Foreign Affairs, Education and Home Affairs have a direct role in the development of a coherent national policy framework. The Department of Foreign Affairs has been proactive in aggressively normalizing relations with countries around the world, the Department of Education has signed a large number of bilateral agreements, while the Department of Home Affairs has been directly involved in the development of policies regarding immigration and study permits for international visitors and students. A policy document proposal, recommending that we formulate a vision of immigration which recognizes that properly managed immigration can be of great economic, social and educational benefit, is being discussed at the present time. There is recognition that the barriers to internationalization must be removed while considering the needs of the country.

At least two other structures of significance in the government sector are the International Relations Directorate in the Department of Education and the International Scientific Collaboration Directorate within the Centre for Science Development (CSD). In the tertiary education sector there are several structures now in place. IEASA aims to promote internationalization in HE and to provide a forum for institutions and individuals to address current issues in the field of international education in South Africa and southern Africa. IEASA plans to be much more than simply a conduit of information by actively engaging in policy development and research.

The South African Universities Vice-Chancellors' Association (SAUVCA) constituted an international relations committee to advise them on, among other things, the extent and importance of international relations for South African universities. This committee met for the first time in October 1997. Similar committees are to be launched by the Committee of Technikon Principals (CTP) and the University and Technikon Public Relations Officers (UNITECH).

Research

South African researchers have failed to keep up with the research demands of technological progress (NCHE 1996: 41). In general the paucity of research may be the result of: lack of research methodology; lack of experience in the South African context; the fact that information was not available in the past; and the fact that local researchers do not yet regard this area of studies as important.

Research is critical if the HE sector is to play an informed and active role in the management of the process of internationalization. Educators need an in-depth analysis of the international dimensions of education; they need to understand the trends and events that likely to influence higher education; they need to know how South African programmes compare in the international competitive market. In the latter case the issue of quality assurance for programmes becomes imperative if we are to continue to attract students from around the world.

In an environment of rapid and unprecedented changes, institutions are also seeking answers to some basic questions to allow them to internationalize in a coherent and professional way. Is globalization merely the rich countries looking after themselves? Will institutions excluded be able to catch up and at what cost? Do the north/south, rich/poor and other divides mean the same thing today or are people more concerned about cultural and other values? If this is so then what are the implications for student mobility? Can we ensure that skills learned locally are applicable globally, and vice versa, to support student and worker mobility? How do we harmonize the local demands and the global challenges? If the statement 'knowledge is power' is now literally true will dangerous conflicts develop between knowledge-rich countries and knowledge-poor countries and institutions?

Conclusion

The international approach must attempt to avoid parochialism in scholarship and encourage research to stimulate critical thinking and enquiry about the complexity of issues and interests that bear on the relations among nations, regions and interest groups. Engaging in international competitiveness does not imply uncritical submission to the forces of globalization. It does, however, require active participation, based on research, and clear national policy. Thabo Mbeki's (1996) hope of an African Renaissance must be tempered by how the government, the private sector and academia can together develop a strategic approach towards being an integral part of Africa and the global community.

References

Castells, M. (1997) The power of identity – the information age. *Economy, Society and Culture* 29–42. Oxford, Blackwell.

Cloete, N., Muller, J., Makgoba, M.W. and Ekong, D. (eds) (1997) *Knowledge, Identity and Curriculum Transformation in Africa.* Cape Town, Maskew Miller Longman.

Daniel, J. (1997) Technology: its role and impact on education delivery: more means better. Plenary address (Theme 5) '*Technology and its Impact on Education Delivery*', 13th Commonwealth Conference of Education Ministers Parallel Convention, Botswana, May.

Department of Education (1995) *First Steps to Develop a New System.* White Paper on Education and Training in a Democratic South Africa, Gazette no. 16312.

Department of Education (1996) *Green Paper on Higher Education Transformation.* Pretoria, Government Printing Service.

Department of Education (1997) *A Programme for the Transformation of Higher Education.* Pretoria, Government Printing Service.

Ekong, D. and Cloete, N. (1997) Curriculum responses to a changing national and global environment in an African continent, in N. Cloete, J. Muller, M.W. Makgoba and D. Ekong (eds) *Knowledge, Identity and Curriculum Transformation in Africa.* Cape Town, Maskew Miller Longman.

Gibbons, M. (1997) International perspectives: a learning experience. Paper delivered at the Inaugural Conference of the International Education Association of South Africa, University of the Western Cape, 29–31 January.

Gourley, B.M. (1997) Managing international relations. Keynote address to the Commonwealth Universities Study Abroad Consortium, University of Sains Malaysia, 6–10 May.

Government Gazette (1995) SAQA Act, Notice 1521, Gazette no. 16725, 4 October.

Haque, S. (1997) '*Globalization of Market ideology and its impact on third world development*' unpublished paper.

Knight, J. (1997) A shared vision? Stakeholders perspectives in the internationalization of higher education in Canada. *Journal of Studies in International Education,* Spring.

Knight, J. and de Wit, H. (1997) Strategies for internationalization of higher education: historical and conceptual perspectives, in H. de Wit (ed.) (1997) *Strategies for the Internationalization of Higher Education: A Comparative Study of Australia, Canada, Europe and the United States of America.* Amsterdam, European Association of International Education.

Kraak, A. (1997) Globalization, change in knowledge production, and transformation of higher education, in N. Cloete, J. Muller, M.W. Makgoba and D. Ekong (eds) *Knowledge, Identity and Curriculum Transformation in Africa.* Cape Town, Maskew Miller Longman.

Mbeki, T. (1996) Opening address by the deputy president of South Africa to the 19th congress of the African National Congress Youth League, 29 February – 3 March.

Mulholland, S. (1997) Interfering government is not doing workers any favours, *Sunday Times*, 9 November.

Naidoo, K. (1997) *Daily News*, 30 December: (Naidoo is an Asia-Pacific analyst at the University of Durban-Westville).

NCHE (National Commission on Higher Education) (1996) *A Framework for Transformation.* Pretoria, Pretoria Department of Education.

Ndebele, N.S. (1997) Paper presented at the International Education Association of South Africa, inaugural conference, University of the Western Cape, January.

Orr, L. (1997) Globalization and universities: towards the 'Market University'? *Social Dynamics*, 23 (1): 42–67.

SADC Human Resources Development Sector (1997) *Protocol on Education and Training.* Pretoria, Department of Education.

Scott, P. (1995) *The Meanings of Mass Higher Education.* Buckingham, Open University Press/SRHE.

Subotzky, G. (1997) Pursuing both global competitiveness and national development: implications and opportunities for South Africa's historically Black universities. *Social Dynamics*, 23 (1): 102–38.

Technology Enhanced Learning Investigation Report (1996) *A Discussion Document: Report of the Ministerial Committees for Development Work on the Role of Technology that will Support and Enhance Learning.* Pretoria: Department of Education.

UNESCO (United Nations Education, Scientific and Cultural Organization) (1992) *Statistical Year Book.* Paris, UNESCO.

Wagner, A. and Schnitzer, K. (1991) Programmes and policies for foreign students and policies for foreign students and study abroad: the search for effective approaches in a new global setting. *Higher Education*, 21 (3): 275–88.

Webster, J. (1997).*Weekly Mail and Guardian*, 23–9. January.

6

A Commonwealth Perspective on the Globalization of Higher Education

Michael Gibbons

Introduction

A perspective on the globalization of higher education (HE) must turn, in the first instance, on some idea of the nature and extent of globalization in the sphere of HE. With regard to the former, globalization is a topic over which there is considerable controversy. The current consensus seems to be that globalization, if it exists at all, is a phenomenon that is still in its early phases, with the exception of investment and possibly some other financial services. In other markets however (motor cars for example) there is still debate over whether supply and demand will call forth a 'world car'. As one scholar has put it recently, the 'cocacolinization' of industry is a dead letter. One cannot conclude, however, that if globalization has not occurred then it is not in process. It may simply be that globalization is proceeding in a very uneven fashion and that trends which can be readily discerned in financial services and to some extent in research and development, particularly in the electronics industry, ought not to be presumed to apply to the same degree in every sector.

Globalization of student exchanges

The question of the globalization of the HE sector, then, must be approached cautiously. Consider, for example, the case of international students. To be sure, there has been an increase in the numbers of international students; that is, students who spend a part of their higher educational formation studying abroad. This trend is clearly evident in the case of Australian universities, in particular, which have made concerted efforts to tap the countries of South East Asia as a source of potential recruits to their HE system. Across the Organization for Economic Cooperation and Development

(OECD), however, the volume of international students does not much exceed 10 per cent. For the most part, the majority of undergraduates are still trained at home, and though many countries have national policies aimed at fostering substantial numbers of international exchanges – Norway, Sweden and the UK, for example – the numbers of students involved are still, relatively speaking, small. Though most countries have scholarship schemes of various sorts, many international students pay their own way. In a few countries – notably Canada, Australia and the UK – international students are now regarded as an important income stream for many universities. Even though the level of mobility among international students is low as a proportion of total students involved in the HE sector, the flows are concentrated in relatively few countries and are of significant financial interest to some of their universities.

More to the point, regarding our concern in this chapter, the flows of students tend to follow lines that have been developed historically, often over a considerable period of time. In Britain, for example, many international students flow along Commonwealth lines from New Zealand, Australia, Canada, India and Africa. Likewise, American students still come to Britain (though fewer than in the past) but as with the Commonwealth connection, this can be traced to the long historical association between the USA and the UK, to the provision of teaching in English, and to the fact many more Americans are either personally wealthy enough or supported by a vast array of US-based scholarships and fellowships to allow them to study abroad for a period of time. Only a few countries (notably Sweden) seem to be investing long term, proactively developing international staff and student exchanges with an eye to future economic relationships.

There are no doubt flows, and possibly increasing flows, of students moving from one country to another in pursuit of HE qualifications but, given the levels involved, it is probably stretching the point to use this as an index of the globalization of HE, even with the proviso that it is an indicator of globalization in an early phase. In particular, it is difficult to determine whether the desire to study abroad will be enhanced or contracted if economic 'globalization' goes further. Somehow, the idea has got about that an economy in which there is already a free flow in the provision of financial services (particularly investment services) will soon exhibit similar patterns across the manufacturing sector, in producer services, and in HE. Perhaps, but not in the short term. The rapid growth in the number of international students is a relatively recent phenomenon but, as we will see below, the special conditions which propelled this growth may be coming to an end.

The reasons for being conservative when forecasting the growth of international students are twofold. First, moving students from one university to another in different countries is very expensive and depends upon the persistence of sufficient economic growth at home to ensure that enough people – largely from the middle classes – have the disposable income to be able to educate their offspring abroad. The recent downturn in the economies of South East Asia provides a good example of how volatile such disposable income can be. Second, with national economic development will come a strengthening of a country's system of HE. In most of the rapidly developing economies of the world the increasing demand for HE is expected to be met through the expansion and improvement of local universities and colleges. The gradual improvement of currently weaker systems of HE means that the globalization of HE is unlikely to take place through enhanced mobility.

Rather than by travelling abroad, it seems far more likely that students will pick up the knowledge they need through some variant of distance learning. Indeed, there are some who maintain that the economics of mass HE provision dictate that this is the way things have to go for all students, not only international ones (Daniel 1996). Here, the current bottleneck is technological, and on the supply side. The technology of delivering mass HE using the techniques of the new information and communication technologies (particularly software applications) is still relatively primitive and, in those cases where the material is excellent (such as the Open University in the UK) the costs of production remain high. No doubt this will change under the pressure of demand for better software. In that case, markets for the provision of courses and degrees through distance learning may come to resemble those that govern international financial dealings currently. But, movement to this stage still waits upon the availability, on-line, of high quality, user-friendly teaching materials.

Globalization of research and development

By contrast with most industrial sectors, the area where globalization seems uncontested is in the sphere of knowledge production. Global flows of information and data seem to be an inherent feature of the emerging knowledge economy. It is in the area of knowledge production – of research – where globalization is most likely to affect HE because universities have successfully styled themselves as producers of 'primary knowledge' and taken the high ground of basic research as their own. But even here there is a tension. Pavitt and others have shown that while ideas, methods and techniques may be produced globally, the innovation process – the development of new products and processes – still takes place locally. While it is true that in the innovation process the required knowledge may, indeed, have been generated in a variety of places, local capability is still essential to be able to bring the various elements to bear on the kinds of concrete problem solving that lead to new products and processes (Pavitt 1991). It is the need to acquire specialized knowledge of all kinds that lies behind the current growth of networks and the proliferation of research and development partnerships and alliances.

These new forms of organization are ostensibly about sharing risk and cost but they are also about getting access to research being carried out by others. Firms want to get value for money out of their expenditures on research but they know that they cannot expect to hold in-house all the knowledge resources that might be needed to maintain their positions in international competition. Therefore, the most efficient way for them to ensure access to new knowledge is by participating in collaborative arrangements of various kinds. As we will try to demonstrate in this chapter, the universities, too, have a key role to play in the emerging knowledge economy but it will be a different role from that which they are now playing.

In what follows, we will restrict ourselves to discussing the globalization of HE from the vantage point of research. The nature of the knowledge environment in which HE will need to operate will be outlined. From this it will become clear that, in future, universities will have to become embedded in a process of knowledge production that, among other things, involves many more participants. Globalization is taking place in the HE sector but is doing so by absorbing universities into a distributed knowledge production system. This will involve the universities in many more alliances and partnerships and will in turn call forth new institutional forms, including new forms of research organization. Finally, we will return to the theme of this chapter and suggest that the new mode of organizing research favours rather than disfavours international groupings such as the Commonwealth.

Some factors affecting the production of knowledge

In the previous section it was suggested that universities are being drawn into a new form of knowledge production system. Before we go on to specify its characteristics more precisely, it will be useful to outline some of the developments that have contributed to the emergence of this new system.

Massification of HE: expansion on the supply side

The massification of HE and the appropriation (after World War II) by the universities of a distinct research function have produced increasing numbers of people familiar with the methods of research, many of whom are equipped with specialized knowledge and skills of various kinds. Massification is now a strongly entrenched phenomenon, is international in scope and is unlikely ever to be reversed. On the supply side, the numbers of potential knowledge producers flowing out of HE is increasing and will continue to do so.

However, this expansion of HE has an implication that has so far been little examined. Not only are an increasing number of people familiar with science and competent in its methods, but also many of these are engaged in activities which have a research dimension. They have brought their knowledge and skills to bear on a wide range of problems in contexts and situations often very remote from the universities where they were originally trained. Scientific and technological knowledge production are now pursued not only in universities but also in industry and government laboratories, in think-tanks, research institutions and consultancies, etc. The expansion of HE internationally has meant that the numbers of places where research is being performed has increased. The implication, not yet fully grasped, is that, to the extent that universities continue to produce quality graduates, they undermine their monopoly as knowledge producers. Many graduates have subsequently become competent to pass judgement on university research and belong to organizations which might do the job just as well. Universities are coming to recognize that they are now only one player, albeit still a major one, in a vastly expanded knowledge production process.

Specialist knowledge: expansion on the demand side

In parallel with this vast expansion in supply has been the expansion of the demand for specialist knowledge of all kinds. The requirement of industry for knowledge, particularly for the results of scientific and technological research, is widely appreciated. The expansion of demand for a flow of specialist knowledge among firms is perhaps less well understood. Specialist knowledge is often a key factor in determining a firm's comparative advantage. As the pressures of international competition increase, firms have tried to meet the challenges presented through the introduction of new technologies. New technology is a necessary but not sufficient condition for successful innovative performance and increasingly, technological innovation depends upon using specialized knowledge to develop technologies in directions dictated by competitive pressures. Specialist knowledge is used partly because it provides a constantly replenishable source of created comparative advantage and partly because it can be difficult to imitate, particularly by firms whose national culture does not yet support a well articulated science and technology infrastructure. Since, in many sectors, these firms represent the spearhead of international competition, specialized knowledge is at a premium but its acquisition is difficult and often too expensive for individual firms to replicate entirely in-house. To meet this exigency firms have become involved in a complex array of collaborative arrangements involving universities, governments and other firms, sometimes from within the same sector. In each case supply and demand are mediated by a market mechanism, but it is not, or need not be, a narrowly commercial one.

In these markets knowledge itself may continuously be sought, but more often than not it is not readily available to be bought or sold, off the shelf, like other commodities. It is increasingly generated in the market nexus itself. In producing specialized knowledge markets operate to configure human and physical resources in a particular context of application. As a consequence of intensifying competition, the numbers of these contexts is expanding but they are also transient. Markets are dynamic. They set new problems more or less continuously and the sites of knowledge production and their associated networks of communication move on. In this context, knowledge is produced by configuring human capital. However, unlike physical capital, human capital is potentially more malleable. Human resources can be configured again and again to generate new forms of specialized knowledge.

Distributed knowledge production

The core of the argument presented here is that the parallel expansion in the numbers of potential knowledge producers on the supply side and the expansion of the requirement of specialist knowledge on the demand side are creating the conditions for the emergence of a distributed knowledge production system. The new system has implications for all the institutions that have a stake in the production of knowledge, especially for universities. The emergence of markets for specialized knowledge means that for each set of institutions the game is changing though not necessarily in the same ways or at the same speed. Some firms and universities are already a long way along the path of change and this is manifested in the types of staff they recruit and in the complex range of collaborative agreements that they enter. However, the institutional goals to be achieved, the rules governing professional development and the social and technical determinants of competence will all need to be modified to the extent that this system becomes established.

The emergence of distributed knowledge production means that specialized knowledge is both supplied by and distributed to individuals and groups across the social spectrum. Communications at institutional levels tend to be bypassed because of the need for rapid, flexible responses to problems. The degree to which current knowledge producing institutions become more permeable will not alter the fundamental fact that knowledge production is taking place in many more types of social setting; that it is no longer concentrated in a relatively few institutions, and involves many different types of individual and organization in a vast array of different relationships.

Distributed knowledge production is tending towards the form of a global web whose numbers of interconnections are being continuously expanded by the creation of new sites of production. As a consequence, communications are crucial. At present communications are maintained partly through formal collaborative agreements and strategic alliances and partly through informal networks backed up by rapid transportation and electronic communications. But this is only the tip of the iceberg. To function, the new mode needs to be supported by the latest that telecommunications and computer technologies have to offer. Distributed knowledge production, then, is both a cause and a consumer of innovations which enhance the flow and transformation of information.

It is one of the characteristics of distributed knowledge production that exploitation of knowledge requires participation in its generation. In distributed knowledge production, the organization of that participation becomes a crucial factor. The goals of participation are no longer simply to secure some national advantage, commercial or otherwise. Indeed, the very notion of what constitutes an economic benefit, and for whom, is at the root of many debates not only in environmental science but in biotechnology and the medical sciences as well. For example, the current push towards 'clean' technologies is about more than just economic benefit. It is also about stabilizing collapsing ecological systems, the health and well-being of populations and commercial gain. This is to say that the distributed production knowledge has co-evolutionary effects in other areas – for example in economics, the prevailing division of labour and our sense of community.

In sum, the key change to note is that knowledge production is becoming less and less a self-contained activity. As practised currently, it is neither the science of the 'universities' nor the 'technology' of industry. It is no longer the preserve of a special type of institution, from which knowledge is expected to spill over, or spin-off, to the benefit of other sectors. Knowledge production, not only in its theories and models but in its methods and techniques, has spread from academia to many different types of institution. It is in this sense that knowledge production has become a distributed process. At its base lies the expansion of the numbers of sites which form the sources for a continual combination and recombination of knowledge resources. What we are seeing is the 'multiplication of the nerve endings of knowledge'.

Briefly, distributed knowledge production has five principal characteristics:

1. There are an increasing number of places where recognizably competent research is being carried out. This can be easily demonstrated by consulting the addresses of the authors of scientific publications, though change is taking place so rapidly that the full extent of the social distribution of knowledge production is probably no longer fully captured by the printed word.
2. These sites interact with one another and thereby continually broaden the base of effective interaction. Thus, contributions to the stock of knowledge are derived from an increasing number of tributarial flows from various types of institution that both contribute to, and draw from, the stock of knowledge.
3. The dynamics of distributed knowledge production lie in the flows of knowledge and in the shifting patterns of connectivity among these flows. The connections may appear to be random but they move with the problem context rather than according either to disciplinary structures or the dictates of national science policy.
4. The number of interconnections is accelerating, so far apparently unchannelled by existing institutional structures. This may be because these connections are intended to be functional and to survive only as long as they are useful. The ebb and flow of connections follow the paths of problem interest, and the paths of problem interest are no longer determined by the disciplinary structure of science.

5. Distributed knowledge production exhibits heterogeneous, rather than homogeneous, growth. New sites of knowledge production are continually emerging which, in their turn, provide intellectual points of departure for further combinations or configurations of researchers. In this sense, the distributed knowledge production system exhibits some of the properties that are often associated with self-organizing systems in which the communication density is increasing rapidly.

In brief, the distributed character of knowledge production constitutes a fundamental change both in terms of the numbers of possible sites of expertise and in their degree of effectiveness in interacting with this distributed knowledge production (Gibbons *et al.* 1994). This will dictate the pace of globalization in HE in the twenty-first century. It is therefore worthwhile exploring some of the main areas where the impact is likely to be great and creative responses needed.

Distributed knowledge production: a new model for universities

Distributed knowledge production is creating a world of collaborative arrangements. Universities that have 'multiplied up' the number of partnerships and alliances in which they are involved and that share their staff and other resources with problem solving teams distributed around the world need to be organized differently. The existence of distributed knowledge production must induce changes in current organizational structures and this is perhaps nowhere so evident than in the perspective that universities will have to take on their intellectual capital.

Heretofore, universities have been seen as 'factories' in which a variety of intellectual capital is employed. Faculty have been specialists, working according to the research practices of disciplinary research. The unit of organization has been the department and graduate students have been the apprentices. Following the dictates of disciplinary research, universities have elaborated the departmental structure and have recruited the best staff they could afford. Universities have often seen themselves as 'owning' this intellectual resource and have used it to establish their reputations *vis-à-vis* one another. Permanent faculty working on specialist topics according to the criteria of 'good science' set down by their disciplines is the arrangement that dominates the university scene, despite the fragmentation that it encourages and the financial resources it requires.

In distributed knowledge production different rules operate. The research agenda is formed and funds are attracted in a different way. Researchers work in teams on problems that are set in a very complex social process and are relatively transient, and move about according to the dictates of problem interest. Participation in these problem contexts is necessary to keep up with what is going on. As a consequence, some of the best academics are tunnelling out of their institutions to join problem configurations of various kinds. To some this is seen as a weakening of loyalty both to their institution and to their discipline. But a new dynamic is at work. If they intend to operate at the leading edge of research, universities need to ensure that faculty are able to participate in the appropriate problem solving contexts. But, these are so diverse and volatile, that no university can afford to keep 'in-house' all the human resources they would need to guarantee a presence everywhere. To maintain a position at the leading edge of research universities need to learn how to exploit all the advantages to be had from sharing their intellectual resources. Here lies a fundamental challenge of distributed knowledge production in the globalizing of HE.

A university set up to exploit the 'economies' of shared resources would seem to require a relatively small core of permanent full-time faculty together with a much larger periphery of other 'experts' that are associated with the university in various ways. As a consequence, the intellectual shape of each university will be much more flexible and better able to adapt to the intellectual demands of new problems. To achieve this, universities will need to experiment with a much wider range of employment contracts, and accept the fact that they will not be able to own outright all the human resources that they need. To an extent this puts the universities in a Catch-22 situation. On the one hand, the demands on universities in terms of both teaching and research is not only growing but it is also diversifying and will continue to do so. To meet this demand universities will need a more diverse complement of intellectual resources. On the other hand, the costs of holding these resources in-house are both too expensive and too inflexible to meet changing demand.

One way out of this dilemma is to make more use of the mutual sharing of resources with others. Vice-chancellors in the future will be distinguished by their ability to utilize their intellectual capital in conjunction with that held by others in a way that maximizes their institutions' goals. They will not presume that every member of staff needs to be a full-time employee. In this case a number of deep structural issues will need to be addressed. For example: how will these 'others' fare in a traditional university setting? How will their contributions be recognized? Will they be promoted? According to what criteria? How much will they cost? How will they relate to graduate students? Will they have to do any teaching? These are some of the questions that need to be asked but it seems clear to me that they cannot be answered without changing the nature of universities substantially.

Universities that wish to participate at the forefront of research will need to participate in distributed knowledge production. To accomplish this, they will, at the very least, have to become more open, porous institutions *vis-à-vis* the wider community, with 'fewer gates and more revolving doors'. They will have to become much more entrepreneurial in the ways that they utilize their 'intellectual' capital, and this may mean experimenting with a much broader range of employment arrangements. But, to the extent that universities go down this road, they may be helping to establish two parallel structures within universities: one which will carry teaching based upon the discipline and another for research (distributed knowledge production). In terms of the processes described above, the emergence of distributed knowledge production will promote the globalization of HE by drawing universities into a much larger knowledge production system. On the other hand, because different structures will be needed within universities to support participation in the new system, there is every danger that teaching and research will gradually become separated.

Transition to the knowledge industries

There is, however, another element to be considered. The distributed knowledge production system in its global dimensions contains a further challenge to HE to provide new types of skill. After all, it is not unreasonable to expect that the emergence of a knowledge economy will need different kinds of 'worker'. And so it appears to be. Important kinds of knowledge are now being produced not so much by scientists or technologists or industrialists as by 'symbolic analysts', people who work with the symbols, concepts, theories, models and data produced by others in diverse locations and configure them into new combinations.

This distinction between 'researchers' who create knowledge and 'symbolic analysts' who configure it underlies that between 'knowledge-based' and 'knowledge' industries. For the most part, knowledge-based industries attempt to understand and improve the operation of a particular manufacturing process. Of course knowledge is produced in the process but researchers are concerned primarily with product and process development. In knowledge-based industries 'products' are still the entities that are bought and sold.

By contrast, for knowledge industries the knowledge itself is the commodity traded. As has been indicated this is now produced in a variety of places – universities, think-tanks, government laboratories – but once knowledge is produced it may be available for reuse in some other combination. In the knowledge industries, value is added by the reiterated use of knowledge, reconfiguring it with other forms of knowledge to solve a problem or to meet a need. Firms in knowledge industries compete with one another in terms of the ingenuity with which they configure knowledge. This resourcefulness is the ultimate source of their created comparative advantage. The massification of HE provides the base from which knowledge industries can emerge. The diffusion of HE through society has had the effect of supplying the continuous flow of trained manpower for the industrial system. Research has already become a central function of the universities – initially in elite institutions, and gradually in others. This process, at first slowly but later with gathering momentum, has not only raised the general level of familiarity with science and technology and the methods and procedures of science but has also multiplied enormously the number of sites where research as a recognizable, professional activity can be carried out. Now, universities need to take a further step and begin training the cadres of knowledge workers whose principal skills and creativity may be associated less with producing new knowledge than with the configuring of knowledge gathered by others.

The special importance of producer services

The role of configured knowledge is particularly evident in the development of producer services which many believe will become the prime source of sustained high added value to sectors as different as high fashion and motor cars. In each case the producer services sector uses specialist knowledge to provide solutions which give products, even mass-produced ones, their specific market edge.

Companies in the producer services sector are organized differently from those in mass-consumption sectors. They have no need of either the large investments or the hierarchical organizations employing large numbers that have characterized mass-production industries. Indeed, such large-scale operations are inimical to the sorts of communication upon which mutual learning occurs and problem solving skills develop. In the producer services sector, data, information and knowledge are the principal commodities traded. By continuously reconfiguring these elements these firms are able to add value to a variety of other products and processes. Their competitive advantage lies in their ability to do this not just once, but again and again.

When the locus of value-added shifts from the creation of knowledge to its configuration, new types of productive workers must emerge to keep the process going. The groups that will give these firms their value will be problem solvers, problem identifiers and problem brokers (Reich 1991). The form of organization in which they will be most productive will not be hierarchical, but will have the capability to handle high-density communications.

The producer services firm, then, takes on some of the characteristics of a spider's web. Each node is a problem solving team possessing a unique combination of skills. It is linked to other nodes by a potentially large number of lines of communication. To survive, each firm must be permeable to new types of knowledge and hence the sector as a whole becomes increasingly interconnected. The interconnections embrace not only other firms but many other knowledge producing groups, be they government research laboratories, research institutes, consultancies or universities. The result, as has been indicated, is a system that has many of the characteristics of distributed knowledge production.

The emergence of producer services represents in our view the early stages of what may one day become known as the knowledge industry. The growth of the producer services sector illustrates the importance of specialist knowledge to all sectors of manufacturing industry as well as the new forms of organization and types of skill required to capture the benefits that customized knowledge has to offer. In this industry, data, information and knowledge are the principal commodities that are sought and value-added, and competitive edge lies in the creativity to configure knowledge resources over and over again. When the emphasis thus shifts from the creation of knowledge to its configuration, new types of productive workers must emerge to drive the process. Reich has identified the groups that give the new enterprise most of its value-added as problem solvers, problem identifiers, and strategic brokers. The form of organization in which they will be most productive will be characterized by low hierarchies and a capacity to handle high density communications. Accordingly, 'messages must flow quickly and clearly if the right solutions are to be applied to the right problems in a timely way. This is no place for bureaucracy' (Reich 1991: 67).

Most importantly for our purposes is the description of how knowledge is created in these organizations. Creative teams solve and identify problems in much the same way whether they are developing new software, dreaming up a new marketing strategy, seeking a scientific discovery or contriving a financial ploy. Most coordination is horizontal rather than vertical. Because problems and solutions cannot be defined in advance, formal meetings and agendas will not reveal them. They emerge instead out of frequent and informal communications among team members. Mutual learning occurs within the team, as insights, experiences, puzzles and solutions are shared: one solution is found applicable to a completely different problem; someone else's failure turns into a winning strategy for accomplishing something entirely unrelated. It is as if team members were doing several jigsaw puzzles simultaneously with pieces from the same pile – pieces which could be arranged to form many different pictures.

Whether you are talking about a project at the forefront of science (the human genome project), technology (fifth generation computer architecture), or a high value enterprise, the organization that carries it looks less like a pyramid and more like a spider's web. This aspect of knowledge production is very well described by Reich and is worth quoting at length:

> Strategic brokers are at the centre, but there are all sorts of connections that do not involve them directly, and new connections are being spun all the time. At each point of connection are a relatively small number of people depending on the task, from a dozen to several hundred. If a group was any larger it could not engage in rapid and informal learning. Here individual skills are combined so that the group's ability to innovate is something more than the simple sum of its parts. Over time, as group members work through various problems and approaches together, they learn about one another's abilities. They learn how they can help one another to perform better, who can contribute what to a particular project, how they can best gain more experience together. Each participant is on the lookout for ideas that will propel the group forward. Such cumulative experience and understanding cannot be translated into standard operating procedures easily transferable to other workers and other organisations. Each point on

the enterprise web represents a unique combination of skills . . . Enterprise webs come in several shapes, and the shapes continue to evolve.
Among the most common are: independent profit centres, spin-off
partnerships, licensing, and pure brokering. The threads of the global
web are computers, facsimile machines, satellites, high-resolution mon-
itors, and modems – all of them linking designers, engineers, contractors,
licensees and dealers world-wide.

(Reich 1991: 91–2)

This description shows very clearly the centrality of specialist knowledge in
the production process and the need for very different forms of organization to capture the benefits that this knowledge has to offer. We have
described this development in terms of the emergence of a new industry to
highlight the fact that, in it, knowledge will be the principal commodity
that is produced and that it will require a new cadre of skills if it is to grow.
New types of organization and styles of management are also required by
high-value enterprises. In particular, they are intrinsically global and will
become more intensely interactive as the telecommunications web diffuses.

In sum, the globalization of the economy and the pressures of international competition are dissolving boundaries between nations, institutions
and disciplines, and giving rise to a distributed knowledge production system. Universities are an integral part of this new system but they are now
only one knowledge producing agency among many in an economic order
where knowledge and skill are central. Through its participation in distributed knowledge production the HE system is also being drawn into the
process of globalization. However, the dissolving effects of international
competition are not the only forces in the field. In particular, political and
cultural forces seem to be militating against the globalizing tendencies of
the economic system which, in turn, are creating a demand for organizations
that successfully bridge these political and cultural divides. The question
which needs to be addressed now is 'What has the development of distributed
knowledge production to do with the Commonwealth?'

A Commonwealth perspective

The question is sometimes asked whether the links created by the Commonwealth have the potential to address the newer and more dynamic
forms of globalization that are emerging. The implication is that existing
links, because they reflect older alignments, are anachronistic, and are perhaps of little use in a globalizing world. It will be clear from what has been
said already about knowledge production and the emergence of the knowledge industry that globalization puts a renewed emphasis on connectivity
and requires linkages of many different kinds. In the knowledge economy,
linkages matter. Concretely, they are sought because of the need to access
knowledge and expertise no matter where it may have been generated.
Linkages are carried and sustained by collaborative organizational forms of

different kinds, including partnerships, alliances and networks. These forms are many and varied and can involve a large number of knowledge producing institutions, not only those in HE. In so far as HE institutions are able, in the sense of having the expertise, to join these problem solving networks, they will become integral to the web of knowledge-based linkages that will be at the heart of the globalization of both the economy and HE.

But there is a paradox at the heart of much of contemporary economic development: along with integration brought about by globalizing markets there has also come the fragmentation of regionalism. The evidence is overwhelmingly present in the vast expansion of trading agreements, organizations and 'blocs' which have emerged across the globe and are essentially regionally based. One does not have to go all the way with the Huntington thesis to appreciate that many of these new arrangements have extra-economic agendas which might play a part in a new configuration of the globe along civilizational and cultural lines (Huntington 1996). Regionalization, whether politically or economically motivated, is a fact of life that is bound to affect the more or less continuous formation of collaborative linkages that are crucial to the type of knowledge production system described above.

The regionalization of economic life may make it more, not less, difficult for knowledge connections to be made across regions, and may inhibit the free flows of knowledge and skill that are implied in globalized problem solving. Distributed knowledge production requires great flexibility and openness in building problem solving capability and the necessary ethos of collaboration may well be inhibited by strengthening cultural groupings along the lines that Huntington has suggested. The solution to the disruptive effects of regionalization will obviously be difficult and complex but the situation creates a special place for those organizations which can bridge regions. Knowledge production follows the lines of problem interest and this interest is bound to reflect economic, political and cultural concerns and well as scientific and technological ones. As ever, brokers are required to create the conditions needed for effective collaboration, and current developments suggest that this may require a significant interregional component.

The Commonwealth comprises an international grouping but its members also belong to other regional organizations and these interconnections have already become especially important. As West (1994: 409) has observed '[in] an increasingly global yet increasingly regionalised economic environment, the Commonwealth's multi-regional membership can be of real economic benefit in facilitating and consolidating bilateral and multilateral trade and investment contacts between and among countries in different economic regions'.

The development of this possibility requires an adjustment in the way the Commonwealth works, or more accurately is perceived to work. In the past, the Commonwealth has typically been conceptualized as an association of member countries acting as an entire group. The development, for example, of the Harare Declaration in 1991 focused on democracy and human rights and was portrayed as an action of the Commonwealth as a whole (McIntyre

1991; Jenkins 1997). But, as West (1994) has convincingly argued, important relationships in the future will often involve collaboration between two, or at most a few, Commonwealth countries on a specific matter – for example, an economic one like trade or investment. The important point that West makes is that apart from the provision of aid:

> economic collaboration between any two Commonwealth countries can be expected to occur without loyalty to the Commonwealth association being one of the reasons. For in the modem global economy, most trade and investment decisions are based upon assessments of comparative economic return. But insofar as a specific trade or investment proposal appears financially sound, commercial collaboration between two Commonwealth countries will certainly be further encouraged by the clear advantages of what could be called a shared Commonwealth business culture.
>
> (West 1994: 410)

Exactly the same argument could be applied to the production of knowledge. In the first instance, experts want to work with other experts. They make commitments to working on complex problems largely in terms of the quality of the people they will be working with. In this, any Commonwealth connection may be secondary. But, in so far as the problem is regarded as important, collaboration between the countries and universities involved will certainly be enhanced by a shared 'Commonwealth university culture'. In HE, years of working together has produced a robust university culture within the Commonwealth which has supported the promotion of teaching and research through international collaboration and exchange. This ought to provide an excellent base on which to build.

Based on a shared English language, shared histories and institutional forms, Commonwealth cultures, whether in business or HE, facilitate the conduct of business and collaboration between Commonwealth countries which in other cultural aspects may be very different. As West (1994: 415) has observed, 'a tendency to separate "economic" and "cultural" factors has sometimes obscured the relevance of the cultural factor in economic decision making'. Yet, close cooperation, whether in economics or research, is normally facilitated by the existence of a common cultural base. In this context, the global reach of the Commonwealth university or business culture has a significance which needs to be more widely acknowledged and carefully analysed. For, regardless of the cultural differences that obviously exist to varying degrees between Commonwealth countries, these shared 'cultures' constitute an important link between them. The Commonwealth connection simply makes it easier to organize the collaboration.

The new element is the crucial contribution of knowledge – particularly, but not exclusively, to economic life. Heretofore, the business and HE cultures have been largely separate. But, as we have seen, the emergence of distributed knowledge production dictates that they now must begin to interact more strongly.

There is a case on efficiency grounds for the closer integration of the Commonwealth business and HE cultures in the emerging knowledge economy. The HE culture in the Commonwealth represents a formidable resource. It is extremely diverse containing within it universities, large and small, carrying out teaching and research in most fields of scholarship. Collectively, it is perhaps the largest and among the wealthiest (both economically and culturally) HE sector internationally, with the exception of the United States. Although academics don't like the association, HE in the Commonwealth constitutes a multi-billion dollar business and at least in the domain of knowledge production universities are now being drawn into a global business.

The globalization of knowledge production in general and the emergence of distributed knowledge production in particular open up fresh possibilities for all universities. As we have seen, right across the economy the lines between HE and the world of industry are becoming blurred. In the knowledge economy, they may well disappear altogether. However, global knowledge production is carried out by teams working in temporary alliances, partnerships and networks, and if the universities are not to be left behind they need to be able to participate in these networks. They need to create structures which will allow them to join in what amounts to a global sharing of resources with others in the distributed knowledge production system. In this framework the globalization of HE will go forwards to the extent and at the speed at which universities are able to connect themselves to the distributed knowledge production system. The distributed system is essentially a system that exploits the benefits to be had from sharing resources.

As is already the case in industry, particularly those branches of it which depend upon knowledge, the future of HE must rely more and more on the extensive use of shared resources. Sharing of resources may be easier within the Commonwealth framework for a number of reasons. First of all, as indicated above, the Commonwealth, in both business and HE dimensions, is a subsystem of the global economy. Both are participating already in the distributed knowledge production system. The imperatives of distributed knowledge production are going to demand many more such collaborative arrangements. And, once a particular alliance is judged to be desirable, it ought to be easier to get concrete working arrangements in place within the framework of Commonwealth relations rather than outside it.

Second, HE is a resource distributed across the Commonwealth and it is already connected by many links and collaborative ties. For example, the universities themselves have been members of a non-governmental organization (NGO), the Association of Commonwealth Universities, for many years and, as a result, existing linkages are strong and of long standing. These linkages are now crucial to the developing knowledge industry and to the preservation of a vibrant research culture in universities. The trick is to extend a network that is already there; to open it to a more diverse range of collaborative partners and arrangements. This is where the Commonwealth university culture could come into its own. By providing the underlying culture from which university–university and university–industry partnerships could grow it would be able to provide models of good practice at the subsystem level, and the Commonwealth connection may well be applicable to the global system as a whole.

Distributed knowledge production depends upon networks. The Commonwealth could show the way forward by developing the network properties of the collective Commonwealth's HE systems and by developing policies to promote the increased used of shared resources, not only among its member universities but between them and other knowledge producers. The network is there, the common institutional forms are there, the familiarity of working with one another is long established. Institutionally, the HE sector of the Commonwealth is well placed to adapt to the emerging model of knowledge production which involves many more partnerships and alliances than previously. The time could be ripe for a more fruitful interaction of the HE and business cultures in the area of knowledge production and configuration.

It should hardly be necessary to add that all the resources needed for any particular collaborative arrangement will not necessarily be drawn from the Commonwealth itself but from the academic community internationally. The world of knowledge production in now global and scientists, as ever, follow the imperative of problem interest which means increasingly that they will work in teams made up of experts from all over the world. To the extent that problem solving teams are drawn from a truly global resource, the degree of interregionality will only increase. The stresses and strains of creating genuinely collaborative structures across regions doesn't go away but they are exacerbated. Again, in this respect, the Commonwealth already has more experience than most in dealing with cross-regional ventures, and could easily develop specific expertise in collaborative research ventures.

So, far from being anachronistic, the Commonwealth – because of its interregional membership – could play a crucial furture role in the area of alliance-building. Despite all the talk of globalization, both HE and business may be about to become increasingly regionalized. If Huntington (1996) is right and there is already evidence of a distinct shift from economic globalism to cultural regionalism, the Commonwealth will be particularly well placed to play a leading interregional role in an increasingly regionalized world.

References

Daniel, J.S. (1996) *Mega-Universities and Knowledge Media.* London, Kogan Page.

Gibbons, M., Limoges, C., Nowotny, H., Schwartzman, S., Scott, P. and Trow, M. (1994) *The New Production of Knowledge: Science and Research in Contemporary Societies.* London, Sage.

Huntington, S.P. (1996) *The Clash of Civilisations and the Remaking of World Order.* New York, Simon & Schuster.

Jenkins, R. (1997) *Reassessing the Commonwealth,* discussion paper no. 72. London, Royal Institute of International Affairs.

McIntyre, W.D. (1991) *The Significance of the Commonwealth: 1965–90.* Canterbury, NZ, Canterbury University Press.

Pavitt, K. (1991) What makes research commercially useful?. *Research Policy,* 20: 109–19.

Reich, R. (1991) *The Work of Nations. Preparing Ourselves for 21st Century Capitalism.* London, Simon & Schuster.

West, K. (1994) Britain, the Commonwealth and the global economy. *The Round Table,* 332: 407–17.

7

The Role of the European Union in the Internationalization of Higher Education

Ulrich Teichler

Institutions of higher education (HE) tend to consider themselves as being international. Many well-established universities already existed before the 'nation state' gained its grip on modern societies (see Briggs and Burn 1985), and academics are more inclined to, and actually do cooperate more internationally than most other professional groups. This state of affairs, however, might have led those responsible within HE institutions to under-estimate the actual extent to which HE in the twentieth century actually was shaped by specific national conditions and national policies. HE is a pre-dominantly national affair today because national policies continuously re-inforce or change the structural and organizational frameworks of the key functions of HE, major research grants are distributed on the national level and course programmes serve predominantly national labour markets. In addition, administrators, academics and students are so much socialized to take the national conditions of HE for granted that they are hardly aware of the extent to which they are national rather than global 'players'.

In observing how HE institutions gradually learn to transcend their na-tional horizon, an analysis of the role of the European Union (EU) is not the most obvious choice. Some observers even claim that Europeanization is not just a small, regional version of internationalization, but rather that regionalization contradicts internationalization by establishing cooperation among neighbours in order to counteract the pressure from more distant regions of the word (cf. the controversial debate in Blumenthal *et al.* 1996). In fact, it is not only the rhetoric frequently employed by EU officials about the rivalry between the United States, Japan and Europe that seems to re-inforce the latter notion, but also the frequent advocacy on the part of the European Commission for strengthening the 'European dimension' in HE.

These observations notwithstanding, many experts seem to agree that the EU actually became a major driving force for internationalization. Ironically, the conflict between efforts on the part of the European Commission to extend constantly its territory of action and the national governments aiming to keep the European Commission out of the core of HE (see Schink 1993) eventually triggered off a European policy of reinforcing grass-root internationalization. Facilitating student mobility became the key instrument for the internationalization of HE.

This chapter aims, after a short introduction on the history of the involvement of the EU in HE, to examine how the goals of the ERASMUS and the subsequent SOCRATES programmes and their actual activities transcend the narrow frame of student mobility, thus contributing to an internationalization of HE institutions at large.

The emerging EU HE policy

The predecessor organizations of the EU were inaugurated with a range of expectations for the reconciliation of countries ravaged by the Second World War. Cooperation in economic regeneration was defined in the three treaties of 1950 focusing on coal and steel, atomic energy and economic cooperation in general among the six founding member countries (France, the Federal Republic of Germany, Italy, The Netherlands, Belgium and Luxembourg). Initial activities centred around the formation of a customs union to remove quotas and other barriers to the free movement of goods, capital, services and people among member states. In this context, educational policy was not a domain in its own right. Rather, reference to education in the original treaties of the EC laid emphasis on vocational training and the mutual recognition of academic qualification in order to facilitate intra-European labour market mobility (see Neave 1984; Opper and Teichler 1989).

By the early 1970s, as the EC's emphasis on a European union was intended to revolve less around economic growth as an end in itself, and more around a broader concern to improve the general quality of life for community citizens whereby the officially sanctioned references to vocational training and academic recognition provided means of entry to the educational arena. Eventually, in 1976, a joint study programmes (JSP) scheme was launched in the domain of HE aiming to stimulate 'cooperation' and 'mobility' (Smith 1979).

The choice of mobility and cooperation as a domain of European policy was not necessarily the most obvious one. Other priorities were discussed and actually striven for, for example efforts to standardize HE curricula in Europe to a certain extent in order to facilitate professional recognition. However, the first efforts of this kind were not successful because the views were too divergent in the various European countries, and most national governments objected to moves towards the 'harmonization' of HE systems. Thus, a consensus was reached to embark on European activities in the area of HE only under the condition that the variety of national HE systems was strictly respected.

The JSPs were aimed at stimulating temporary study in partner departments, teaching staff exchange and joint developments of programmes or parts thereof. In reality, student mobility became the major and most visible activity. After almost ten years of experience gathered from these pilot schemes, evaluation studies came to the conclusion that close cooperation, substantial administrative and academic support as well as a substantial degree of curricular integration had been developed in the majority of programmes (see Dalichow and Teichler 1986; Baron and Smith 1987). The success of such a programme was viewed as more likely if financial support for the HE institutions was not limited to a few years and if the European Commission did not merely focus their support on the HE institutions, but rather established a supplementary fellowship system for covering the additional costs of study in another European country. In 1987, the ERASMUS programme was founded – a programme which focused on student mobility and included various other means of cooperation. It grew within less than ten years to the size of more than 100,000 mobile students per year, and it became generally viewed as the most successful of more than a dozen educational programmes the European Commission had established in the latter half of the 1980s (see the overview in European Commission 1994).

Student mobility was not the most obvious choice for a European policy, because student mobility formed part of a vertical relationship. Students from poor countries with at most low-quality HE went to rich countries with stable HE systems. Within developed countries students tried to improve their knowledge by moving for some period – most likely that of advanced study – to the most prestigious institutions in their discipline. Student mobility, therefore, tended to be one-way rather than reciprocal (see Baumgratz-Gangl 1996: 105). In contrast, student mobility within the European Community was intended to be reciprocal and on-par in principle, even though this was not achieved for all exchanges.

The ERASMUS programme was clearly the core programme addressing HE in the European Community. However, there were other programmes also relevant to HE. The COMETT programme, established in 1986, aimed to promote cooperation between education and industry. The LINGUA programme, established in 1989, was responsible for the promotion of language teaching and learning. The 'Action Jean Monnet' allowed the establishment of European teaching-staff positions, and the TEMPUS programme aimed to support cooperation with institutions of HE in Central and Eastern Europe.

In the Treaty of Maastricht, which came into force in 1993, education became a regular task of the European Community, thereafter called the EU: 'The Community shall contribute to the development of quality education by encouraging cooperation between Member States and, if necessary, by supporting and supplementing their action' (Article 126.1). 'Developing the European dimension in education' was set as a new major target. The activities should, however, be undertaken within clear limits and should:

'fully respect the responsibility of the Member States for the content of teaching and the organization of education systems and their cultural and linguistic diversity'; 'exclude any harmonization of the laws and regulations of the Member States'; and have a subsidiary function, i.e. be undertaken only if they could not be successfully undertaken by the member states themselves.

In the mid-1990s, the EU regrouped and extended its educational programmes. SOCRATES became the umbrella programme for education, and ERASMUS was basically preserved and became the largest sub-programme. There were some changes, though, in the support for institutions of HE which were relevant for their international approach, and these will be discussed below. LEONARDO became the umbrella programme for vocational education and links to industry, whereby various elements of the COMETT programme were continued. In the context of these changes, the educational budget of the EU was enlarged, but still remained below 1 per cent of the overall budget of the EU.

De-nationalization of curricula

The support for student mobility in the framework of ERASMUS, embedded in various forms of administrative and academic support, and combined with support for the development of programmes or parts thereof, is clearly a means for curricular change. One could even claim that support for student mobility was not meant as an end in itself, but rather a means only to induce curricular change. According to this view, the instrument of student mobility was primarily chosen because it was the only legitimate way of inducing substantial curricular change without obvious disregard of the required respect for the variety of HE systems and for the prerogative of the national governments to shape those systems. If joint European and international approaches had to stop in front of national barriers, the support of networks of departments is an obvious means of creating common curricular elements within departments, thus weakening national powers of curricular coordination (governments, professional associations, academics cooperating on a national basis, etc.). After a period, the multitude of transnational networks could denationalize curricula and the curricular map of Europe would no longer be comprised of nations but rather of an abundance of cooperating networks.

This view, however, cannot be confirmed clearly, because the European Commission could not pursue such a policy overtly. It is obvious, though, that student mobility was embedded in a multitude of direct or indirect curricular means and that many departments participated initially in the JSPs and subsequently in the ERASMUS scheme. Some examples follow.

When the European Commission and isolated European countries (for example the Federal Republic of Germany, and Sweden) began to support collective student mobility, they copied many experiences of the American international student exchange programmes established after the Second

World War. However, they opted for a single clear distinction: collective student mobility – arranged between American institutions of HE through cooperation between the institutions at large and organized by central international offices – was given into the hands of cooperating departments in Europe. This European approach was clearly meant to underscore the relevance of the academic dimension of study abroad and to stimulate cooperation in curricular as well as teaching and learning matters. A survey undertaken in the 1980s shows that those responsible for student exchange programmes at American universities appreciate more highly the *cultural* value of study abroad than their European counterparts. In fact, both the American coordinator and the students themselves observe a stronger cultural impact as a result of study abroad than the European coordinators and students. In reverse, those responsible for student exchange programmes in European countries (including those involved in JSP) regard the *academic* value of study abroad more highly than their American colleagues, and, again, both the European coordinators and students perceive a stronger academic impact of study abroad than their American counterparts (Teichler and Steube 1991).

The JSPs scheme provided only marginal support for mobile students. 32 per cent of the JSPs did not involve in student exchange at all. Almost half of the JSPs were active in teaching-staff exchange and in the production of teaching material (Commission of the European Communities 1985: 13). Many of those responsible for cooperation in the cooperating networks stated that the partner departments cooperated closely in curricular matters. This served in a substantial number of cases merely to identify the most suitable courses to be studied abroad; in many cases, however, joint efforts were undertaken to revise the courses. Cooperation went so far in the framework that a joint degree (i.e. a degree both from the host and the home institution) was awarded to all students upon completion of studies in 13 per cent of the networks, and in a further 19 per cent of the programmes was awarded to students fulfilling certain requirements or eventually taking additional exams (Dalichow and Teichler 1986: 75).

When EC support for mobility and cooperation was put on a large-scale footing with the establishment of the ERASMUS scheme, a drop in the proportion of networks strongly emphasizing curricular integration was likely. Networks applying for ERASMUS support were not formally required to strive for curricular integration. However, evidence had to be provided that recognition was likely upon return for the study achievements during the period abroad, and the Commission made clear through reports about selection criteria or on 'good practice' that preparatory courses for the study abroad programmes, academic and administrative support for incoming ERASMUS students and steps towards curricular integration were expected. Among those responsible in the individual departments in 1991/2 for ERASMUS activities, 8 per cent reported that a joint degree was awarded and 10 per cent that a joint certificate was handed over to the students upon successful completion of study (Teichler and Maiworm 1997: 81).

Many of those responsible for ERASMUS activities reported that students turned out to be 'change agents'. Students, as a rule, observed major contrasts between curricula, teaching and learning modes, examination practices, administrative procedures as well as the social environment and institutional cultures between their host and their home institution of HE. The ERASMUS student surveys of 1988/9 and the 1990s – showed through the aggregation of responses to countries, for example – that the European students appreciated the academic quality in Denmark, Germany and The Netherlands, as well as the student-centred and communicative approaches of HE in the United Kingdom and Ireland. In contrast, they were most impressed by the customs and traditions in Spanish and Portuguese society (see Maiworm *et al.* 1991). More importantly, however, the students reported upon return their experiences at the host institutions, and incoming students often let their host know how they perceived the life and study conditions at the host institution. This feedback from intra-European student exchange was often reported as having been eye-opening and has certainly stimulated efforts for improvement.

Europeanization or internationalization of curricula

According to official EU documents, the aim underlying the support of cooperation and mobility in HE is clearly to promote 'European' awareness and cooperation. They do not refer to the 'international' dimension of HE at all. It remains deliberately open whether promotion of European cooperation and mobility reinforces or contradicts the international approach of HE institutions.

Among the networks most active in student exchange in the past, we noted those focusing on Europe in terms of knowledge of European Community law or policies or in terms of fostering knowledge about various European countries and their interactions – for example, 'European business'. A close look, however, revealed that very few study programmes with 'European' in their title were confined to the European Community. Danthony (1995) provided evidence that only 35 study programmes at German institutions of HE were in the strict sense either addressing the arrangements of the EU or EU member states, of which almost all were located at *fachhochschulen*. In contrast, almost all European business studies, area studies, foreign language programmes etc. at universities were broader in scope, embracing all European cultures (or all cultures shaped by Roman languages, i.e. including, at least in principle, Latin America, Francophone Africa, etc.).

Most departments involved in ERASMUS clearly emphasized an international rather than a European approach. They appreciated European support and a growing number of students from neighbour countries, but neither conceptually nor pragmatically did they wish an exclusive emphasis on Europe. Two figures indicate that an exclusive European approach is unlikely from a pragmatic point of view: one-third of the departments involved in a network supported by ERASMUS (the so-called inter-university cooperation programmes) sent out one or two students per year, and a further third sent out between three and five students (Teichler and Maiworm 1997: 25). Even if we take into account that some departments were involved in more than one inter-university cooperation programme, large-scale student mobility between departments was not frequent.

On the other hand, institutions of HE involved in ERASMUS in 1994 reported that ERASMUS students comprised on average only 11 per cent of their foreign students (Maiworm *et al.* 1996: 53). Therefore, we conclude that an exclusive European emphasis in the academic and administrative arrangements for incoming students would cause in most cases more problems than it would resolve.

From a conceptual point of view, occasional conversations with those responsible for the ERASMUS programme within institutions of HE clearly confirm that most academics not confined in national settings consider themselves international or cosmopolitan rather than European or regional. Also, we permanently came across the question of what 'the European dimension' means at all. Similarly, most students seem to appreciate study in another European country primarily for having experiences contrasting to those at home. Very few seemed to be interested in exploring common elements across Europe. If Europe played a role, it provided contrasts on a softer basis – less costly, less risky and less exotic than in the framework of mobility to countries outside Europe.

A provisional summary

Undoubtedly, ERASMUS is generally viewed as a success story. Of course, one can point to many problems. For example:

- The initial aim of supporting 10 per cent of European students through this scheme (i.e. about 2.5 per cent each year in study programmes lasting on average about four years) has not been achieved, because the member states are not willing to extend the educational budget correspondingly.
- Complaints grow among students over the years that the scholarships do not cover the additional costs for studying abroad.
- The participating departments and institutions complain about the red tape involved, and the students are annoyed by the fact that they get to know the award decision, as a rule, only shortly before their scheduled departure to the host country, and most of them receive financial support only some time after they go abroad.
- It is worth noting that only half the number of students initially named in the applications actually go abroad (Teichler and Maiworm 1997: 30). Of course, some participating departments and institutions might deliberately exaggerate the number of possibly mobile students, hoping that the

inflated number might improve their chances of being awarded substantial support. However, this statistic is an indicator that often the actual number of mobile students is substantially lower than their departments had initially expected.

- The recognition of study achievements abroad upon return are lower than one might wish. Former ERASMUS students believe that their overall study period was on average prolonged due to the study period abroad by about 40 per cent of the duration of the study period abroad.

Given this range of problems, it is all the more noteworthy that ERASMUS is generally viewed as a success story. This clearly indicates that some aspects of ERASMUS are extraordinarily highly regarded. On the basis of the evaluation studies undertaken, we tend to conclude that ERASMUS caused a breakthrough in transferring an international scope of teaching and learning from an exceptional to a regular and normal element of study at most institutions of HE, even if international student mobility remained confined to a minority of less than 10 per cent. The major effect of the programme was not to provide international experience to 100,000 students, but to change the substance and modes of learning for millions by comparatively small financial and marginal regulatory means. The European Commission, while talking about Europe, is a powerful actor of internationalization, whereby Europe is actually predominantly a sub-category of less than systematic relevance. The Commission's contribution to internationalization rests primarily on its successful challenge to national forces of curricular coordination. In its de-nationalizing effect on curricula and its provision of opportunities for European students to experience academic and cultural contrast in another country, Europeanization à la ERASMUS coincides with internationalization.

Towards an institutional European or international strategy

Since 1996, institutions of HE have applied for ERASMUS, within the framework of SOCRATES, under new rules. On the one hand, the areas of support have shifted. A higher proportion of the budget than in the past is reserved for teaching staff mobility, in order to increase the benefits of ERASMUS to non-mobile students, and in order to achieve curricular, teaching and learning reforms. On the other hand, the major changes to ERASMUS within the framework of SOCRATES are of a managerial nature. To qualify for support from the academic year 1997/8 onwards:

- each institution of HE has to submit a single application encompassing all its exchange and cooperation activities, thus replacing the previous pattern of submission of application by networks of departments;
- institutions have to provide evidence about the soundness of the cooperative activities named in the application by means of contractual evidence

that they have signed bilateral cooperation agreements with other institutions of HE;

- each institution submitting an application is obliged to submit a European policy statement (EPS) which is expected to present the overall concept underlying their actual and envisaged European activities and the role SOCRATES support is supposed to play in this framework.

These managerial changes generally amounted to more salient changes than a mere shift in bureaucratic procedures. SOCRATES challenges the institutions of HE to:

- reflect and put a stronger emphasis on the coherence of goals to be pursued and the coherence of European activities to be undertaken;
- strengthen the responsibility of the central level of the HE institutions regarding European activities, notably in taking priority decisions, providing a support structure and ensuring the resource basis for European activities;
- develop and reinforce strategic thinking in terms of setting clear targets and pursuing them successfully.

This change of the ERASMUS approaches within SOCRATES was initially met with widespread reservations and criticisms. On the one hand, fear was expressed that academics would not be interested in student mobility and related curricular innovations if they lost their dispositions, their direct access to the financial means provided and the opportunity to regularly visit their partners and cooperate in improving the internationalization process through face-to-face contacts. On the other hand, doubts were raised as to whether the range and quality of mobility and cooperation addressed in ERASMUS depended substantially on the strategic approach of a given HE institution.

A recent evaluation study (not yet published) undertaken by the Association of European Universities in cooperation with the Centre for Research on Higher Education and Work at the University of Kassel shows that the initial reservations persisted in some respects in 1997 when the first application within the new framework was filed and when the institutions received the first rewards in this framework, but that the reactions were later somewhat modified.

The study first suggests that a surprisingly high proportion of HE institutions applying for SOCRATES support eventually perceived the need to formulate an EPS as a useful exercise to reflect their past and future international policies and the role SOCRATES support could play in this context. Also, many institutions rearranged and formalized their European responsibilities, thus making sure that daily decisions on international activities were embedded in their overall policies and activities.

Second, most institutions appreciated an extension of ERASMUS support in favour of teaching staff mobility and curricular innovation, if substantial additional resources were made available, but clearly not at the price of reducing or lowering the quality of student mobility. It was felt necessary to keep the key strength of the old network approach: close cooperation among academics in order to facilitate and intensify curricular integration and coordination which was likely to improve the quality of learning abroad and the extent or recognition upon return.

Third, most institutions did not regard student mobility as an area in which they needed to target priorities, but rather tried to ensure the maximum take-up. A targeted priority seemed to be more feasible and desirable in the domain of curricular innovation and possibly in the domain of teaching staff mobility, serving predominantly the non-mobile students.

Fourth, many of the respondents to the evaluation study obviously expected the European Commission to be itself more consistent in its efforts to stimulate strategic thought and action if it wanted to have a major impact on HE institutions in this direction. The Commission was seen as a facilitator of a European strategy by HE institutions only if, in making awards, the EPS was treated not merely as a prerequisite but as a key element in the application and so influential in determining whether an award was made or not. Also, strategic thought and action were considered more likely to be stimulated if the Commission did not only provide support for a substantial list of clearly prescribed activities, but named larger and more open territories in which the institutions of HE could strive for innovations beneficial for Europeanization and internationalization.

In this context, the question deserves attention as to whether this stimulation of a strategic approach actually moves the institutions more strongly towards developing a set of goals and activities which could be viewed as European in terms of being distinct from 'international', or towards Europeanization which more or less coincides with internationalization. In seeking to respond to this question, one could take into account EPS vocabulary. Actually, 'European' goals clearly dominate 'international' goals, according to the EPS rhetoric. A closer look reveals, however, that in the majority of cases where reference to Europe dominates, a clear link between 'European' and 'international' is expressed. Apart from a minority of less than 20 per cent of the cases, a 'European' policy is either viewed as part of an international policy or at least not as a contradiction to an international policy.

It would be premature to say whether SOCRATES in fact stimulates a substantial leap forward in the direction of strategic institutional behaviour towards European and international activities. One has to bear in mind that the evaluation study focused on processes of deliberation prior to the first year of activities supported by SOCRATES. Also, the HE institutions tended to believe, in the process of formulating their EPS, that more money would be made available for new activities than actually was awarded. Widespread disappointment might reduce the readiness of strategic reasoning in the future. Finally, it has yet to be seen whether the actual activities supported by SOCRATES will turn out to be comprehended as a configuration shaped by strategy.

It is interesting to note in this context that many institutions of HE intend to broaden the number and the range of countries to be involved in the kind of activities SOCRATES supports. Many references were made in this context to the Central and Eastern European countries, some of which will soon join SOCRATES. In most of the cases in which explanations for this desired extension of cooperation were provided, the institutions favoured an extension of countries involved in student mobility and institutional cooperation, teaching staff exchange and curricular innovation in general rather than emphasizing a pan-European approach. Altogether, the most recent observations again support the view that the European HE programmes are very successful tools for the continuous internationalization of HE institutions. This success seems to be endangered only if the member states of the EU opt, in shaping the future of SOCRATES at the beginning of the next millennium, for a more narrow concept of 'Europeanization'.

References

Baron, B. and Smith, A. (eds) (1987) *Higher Education in the European Community: Study Abroad in the European Community.* Luxembourg, Office for Official Publications of the European Communities.

Baumgratz-Gangl, G. (1996) Development in the internationalisation of higher education in Europe, in P. Blumenthal, C. Goodwin, A. Smith and U. Teichler (eds) *Academic Mobility in a Changing World*, pp. 103–28. London and Bristol, PA, Jessica Kingsley.

Blumenthal, P., Goodwin, C., Smith, A. and Teichler, U. (eds) (1996) *Academic Mobility in a Changing World.* London and Bristol, PA, Jessica Kingsley.

Briggs, A. and Burn, B.B. (1985) *Study Abroad: A European and an American Perspective.* Paris, European Institute of Education and Social Policy.

Commission of the European Communities (1985) *Conference on Higher Education Co-operation in the European Community, Brussels 27–29 November 1985: Conference Document.* Brussels, Office for Co-operation in Higher Education.

Dalichow, F. and Teichler, U. (1986) *Higher Education in the European Community: Recognition of Study Abroad in the European Community.* Luxembourg, Office for Official Publications of the European Communities.

Danthony, M-J. (1995) *Europäische Studiengänge in der Bundesrepublik Deutschland: Ein Modell der Europäisierung der Hochschulbildung.* Dissertation, Universität Bremen.

European Commission (1994) *Co-operation in Education in the European Union 1976–1994* ('Education, Training, Youth, Studies' no. 5). Luxembourg, Office for Official Publications of the European Communities.

Maiworm, F., Steube, W. and Teichler, U. (1991) *Learning in Europe: The ERASMUS Experience.* London and Bristol, PA, Jessica Kingsley.

Maiworm, F., Sosa, W. and Teichler, U. (1996) *The Context of ERASMUS: A Survey of Institutional Management and Infrastructure in Support of Mobility and Co-operation.* Kassel, Wissenschaftliches Zentrum für Berufs- und Hochschulforschung der Universität Gesamthochschule Kassel.

Neave, G. (1984) *The EEC and Education.* Stoke-on-Trent, Trentham Books.

Opper, S. and Teichler, U. (1989) European Community (EC): educational programmes, in T. Husén and T.N. Postlethwaite (eds) *The International Encyclopedia of Education, Supplementary Volume One,* pp. 342–7. Oxford, Pergamon.

Schink, G. (1993) *Kompetenzerweiterung im Handlungssystem der Eurpäischen Gemeinschaft: Eigendynamik und 'Policy Entrepreneurs'. Eine Analyse am Beispiel von Bildung und Ausbildung.* Baden-Baden, Nomos.

Smith, A. (1979) *Joint Programmes of Study: An Instrument of European Co-operation in Higher Education.* Luxembourg, Office for Official Publications of the European Communities.

Teichler, U. and Maiworm, F. (1997) *The ERASMUS Experience: Major Findings of the ERASMUS Evaluation Project.* Luxembourg, Office for Official Publications of the European Communities.

Teichler, U. and Steube, W. (1991) The logics of study abroad programmes and their impacts. *Higher Education,* 21 (3): 325–49.

8

Globalization and Concurrent Challenges for Higher Education

Jan Sadlak

A cautiously optimistic vision of the future of the world can be summarized as follows: 'The society that mankind will inhabit in the 21st century is being shaped by new and powerful forces that include the globalization of economic activity, the growing importance of knowledge as a prerequisite for participation in fundamental human activities and the increasing democratization of political systems' (UNESCO 1997: 7). Education, in general, and higher education (HE), in particular, has been an important factor in laying the foundations for such an evolution of society. It is expected that HE will play a prominent role also with regard to globalization and how this concept will evolve. Will globalization be a starting point for a more coherent vision of global problems and a more equitable use of what we all produce and consume, or it will be the epitome of the globalized *laissez-faire* flow of capital, goods, entertainment and information?

Whatever specific characteristics we tend to associate with the concept of 'globalization', it is an expression of 'new geopolitics' in which a control over territory is of lesser importance than the control of and access to all kinds of markets, the ability to generate and use knowledge and the capacity to develop new technology and human resources. As such, 'globalization' becomes not only a complex interlinking of various (and not only economic) processes but also a sombrely dominant framework for anxious peering into our future as individuals and members of society. This chapter tries to look, foremost from the global perspective, at how the recent developments, still persisting imbalances, changing conditions and challenges facing HE can relate to this irreversible but not yet conclusively positive prospect for internationalization in the years to come.

Quantitative paradigm

The mounting statistics on student population attest to the fact that extraordinary effort is being expended on a global scale in expanding the HE enterprise. All societies, whether modern or modernizing, post-industrial or developing, are experiencing increasing demand for access to HE, foremost in order to respond to an increasing requirement for trained citizens for an economy which more and more depends upon knowledge-related skills and the ability to handle information. Without assuming monopoly, only HE institutions can produce such citizens in big numbers and of varied kinds.

The number of students in HE in the world increased from 51 million in 1980 to about 82 million in 1995, representing an increase of 61 per cent. In a majority of highly industrialized countries, around 50 per cent of the typical HE-bound age group of 18–23 are enrolled in various types of HE institution. According to data from the World Bank, there is a clear correlation between the level of participation in HE and economic development, which on average is 51 per cent in the Organization for Economic Cooperation and Development (OECD) countries, compared with 21 per cent in middle-income countries and 6 per cent in low-income countries (World Bank 1994). On a worldwide basis the overall ratio has increased from 12.2 per cent in 1980 to 16.2 per cent in 1995.

A closer look at the pace with which the process of transformation from a relatively elitist to a mass HE system took place is also worthwhile. For example, in 1955 in France there were less than 150,000 students. Today, there are about 2,169,000 students which represents more than 46 per cent of 18–23 age group. In Germany, student numbers have increased by 80 per cent since 1977. At present, the number of students exceeds such coveted professional/social groups as farmers in a majority of OECD countries. All these are signs of enormous systemic changes in which demography plays an important but not a decisive role.

By no means is this trend limited to highly industrialized countries. For example, in the last 25 years the number of students in HE in Saudi Arabia increased more than 21 times. Many rapidly developing countries, especially those in South East Asia, plan to increase the proportion of school-leavers going into HE to levels which would be similar to those of the most advanced countries. The same tendency is observable also in most countries of Central and Eastern Europe where the level of participation in HE is still below the 30 per cent mark.

At present, in some 20 countries the number of students enrolled in HE exceeds 1 million. Of these 20, at least half are developing countries. And this has been achieved only in the course of last decade or so. The similarity of the pace of this development with that of urban growth in those countries is quite striking.

However, when presenting these trends, it is also necessary to bear in mind the still existing inequality of access to HE between various countries and regions. It must be recalled that despite the progress achieved in this area, young people's opportunities to pursue HE in sub-Saharan Africa are 17 times lower than in the industrially developed countries, nowadays often described as 'the North', and are on average four times lower for young people in *all* the developing countries. (The end of communism as a global ideological force and the end of the East–West confrontation brought about changes in the configuration of the so-called regions. It resulted in the world being seen in a bipolar configuration in which the countries which belong to the non-aligned movement, together with developing countries, have reoriented themselves to be become the South, while the rest of the countries, especially those in Europe and North America, have been grouped to become the North. The ascendance of the trading blocs has only reinforced this perspective.)

Overall, the policy of wide access to HE is nowadays more a rule than an exception. The argument for the continuation of this policy is based, among other things, on estimations concerning the evolution of labour markets which show that in the course of the next decade some 40 per cent of all jobs in the industrialized countries will require 16 years of schooling and training. For the developing countries the argument is similar as it looks as if one of the characteristics of the next century will be further internationalization of economic relations and further development of technology. To this end it is almost an imperative that more and more people must master science and technology as well as information.

Already in the late 1970s, James Perkins, for many years the chairman of the International Council for Educational Development (ICED) and the former president of Cornell University, in a lucid analysis of principal axioms determining the quantitative development of HE, noted that 'in every society entry to higher education must be open to a minimum percentage of the entering age group if that society is to grow and survive. This percentage varies according to different opinions, but it would seem that a range of between 12 and 18 per cent of the age group constitutes a reasonable number'. He also gives a stern warning that 'Any society that does not give at least 12 per cent of the age group access to post-secondary education does not have a chance to survive in the type of future that lies ahead' (Perkins 1977: 134). It is worth keeping in mind arguments brought by Perkins when, under a banner of due concern for priority and efficiency of educational investment, the role of HE is de-emphasized.

Informational paradigm

In the context of the topic of this chapter, it is hard to omit new information and communication technology which gives a practical dimension to being 'global' and not only with regard to HE. The greatest contributor to rapid multi-faceted globalization which can be most directly attributed to academia is probably the Internet, which was developed as a result of researchers' desire for rapid and low-cost communication. In the course of recent years it has become a powerful economic and cultural instrument. Together with other wonders of new information and telecommunication technology, we are rapidly observing profound changes in the way students acquire knowledge and scientists carry out their work and communicate among themselves on local, national and international levels.

The term 'university without walls' which was often used in the 1970s to promote not only new educational technology but also the idea of political and cultural openness in HE becomes a pragmatic high-tech reality, symbolized by another term – the virtual university. The number of such virtual institutions offering virtual degrees is steadily increasing. According to some estimates, in the United States alone there are about 300 colleges and universities offering this form of HE studies and over 1 million students are now plugged into the virtual classroom. It is also estimated that the number of 'cyberstudents' will more than triple by the turn of the century. There are more and more signs that distant and traditional forms of studying are merging and mutually supplementing each other. Besides offering an alternative means of getting a degree, this type of studying can be an effective form of providing retraining and upgrading of courses without involving too much of a break from professional employment or time-consuming travel to the campus. In order to be able to take full advantage of marvellous informational tools, members of the academic community must not only have the right equipment but continue to develop their symbolic analytical skills.

There is no need to worry that the traditional academic work of teaching, studying and research in a conventional institution of HE is going to disappear altogether. Being together and talking to other students, teachers and researchers is going to be an academically and socially essential part of intellectual and professional development for as long as we can forsee. There is however no doubt that virtual education is an alternative to mainstream provision of HE. Some argue that it also will bring sorely needed competition to conventional HE. It might also be an answer when dealing with still unmet demand for HE, particularly in the developing countries, because, as John Daniel, the vice-chancellor of the Open University argues, 'Merely to keep student participation rates constant in the developing world, one sizeable new university has to open every week to meet the demands of the young and growing population' (Daniel 1996: 14). Obviously, in a situation where very few developing countries can afford to fund at appropriate levels already existing HE institutions, new technology can be a logical option. What remains problematic is how much those countries will be able to sustain their indigenous knowledge capacity in order to be able to produce educational software adequate to their own needs. It should also be pointed out that the globalized circulation of information might not be an all-inclusive partnership, especially in those cases when academic recognition and traditional not-for-profit circulation of knowledge within the academic community will be replaced by 'for-profit' activities.

International versus global university cooperation

It is not too presumptuous to claim that there is more 'international content' within an average university than within a transnational, globally operating corporate organization. This derives from the very nature of HE learning and academic work which imposes the seeking of relevance and confirmation not only on local or national but also on global levels. The long history of the universities shows that intellectual self-sufficiency and inward-looking parochialism lead to a decline of HE and its institutions. A desire to know and understand 'others' brings many people to the doors of universities. A growing number of HE institutions articulate in their mission their commitment to internationalization. This takes a multitude of forms which makes assessing them, particularly at the supra-institutional level, quite difficult, with the exception of international student mobility.

According to recent studies by the United Nations Educational, Scientific and Cultural Organization (UNESCO), in 1995 more than 1.5 million foreign students were enrolled for HE study in the 50 major host countries. More than 800,000 students from less developed regions were enrolled for third-level study in a foreign country, as were more than 150,000 students from the former communist countries of Central and Eastern Europe and Euro-Asian countries of the former Soviet Union. About 440,000 students from more developed regions were enrolled for HE in another country.

If this aspect of internationalization of HE is a remarkable development, the pattern of student flows across national boundaries has hardly become more globally balanced. As in past years, more than three-quarters of all foreign study takes place in just ten host countries: the United States (more than 30 per cent of all foreign students), France (more than 11 per cent), Germany (about 10 per cent), the United Kingdom (about 9 per cent), the Russian Federation (about 5 per cent), Japan (more than 3 per cent, i.e. 3.5 per cent), Australia (about 3 per cent), Canada (less than 2.5 per cent), Belgium (less than 2.5 per cent) and Switzerland (about 2 per cent), followed by two other countries, Austria and Italy, with almost the same number of foreign students as Belgium, at around 25,000. With the exception of one, all these 'host countries' are members of the OECD, once again confirming the direct correlation between economic strength and the capacity of educational and scientific systems.

A number of countries have adopted a policy of increasing their international student population. As a result of this decision, countries such as Germany, the United Kingdom, Japan and Australia reported an increase of more than 10 per cent. It is worth pointing out that the most rapid growth took place in China where the number of foreign students increased by more than 27 per cent, from 3250 in 1985 to 22,617 in 1995.

It is much less encouraging to see a continuous imbalance of participation with regard to student mobility in sub-Saharan African countries. With the exception of South Africa, no other country of this region is among the 50 major host countries. And when analysing the number of students abroad as a percentage of national enrolment, once again, only one country – Cameroon – is among the group of 50 'major countries of origin'. It can be argued that if a national system of HE responds sufficiently to student demand then there is no need to undertake study abroad. This would be an encouraging conclusion but it is more likely that this situation is the result of the generalization of poverty in and the declining financial capacity of those countries to send their nationals to study abroad. As a result, they reduce their collective capacity to develop a deeper understanding of cultures, technologies, languages and business methods, or to build personal networks. Long seen as a plus for intellectual and cultural diversity, foreign students have now become a part of 'economic competitiveness' in the global economy. It is the very reason why such an organization as the European Commission has launched well-structured and relatively well-founded student mobility schemes such as ERASMUS and SOCRATES which allowed some 500,000 students in member states of the EU to spend a meaningful period of their studies in another country of the European Union. Other organizations or treaties such as the NAFTA, ASEAN, APEC and Mercorsur encourage student mobility within their member states. There is a risk that despite globalization or maybe because of it, we might move away from multilateral cooperation towards more controllable bilateral co-operation. This would sooner rather than later lead to a significant number of members of the international community being excluded from active participation in the globalized economy, international scientific and cultural exchanges, etc.

There tends to be a strong conviction that one means of better preparing future graduates for the demands of an increasingly international, professional life is to provide them with more opportunities to study and live abroad. The personal, educational and ultimately social benefits are difficult to measure but it is often acknowledged that studying abroad results in:

- acquiring new knowledge and competencies;
- inproving knowledge of a foreign language;
- familiarization with new teaching methods as well as new scientific equipment, organization of laboratories, etc.;
- opportunities to purchase new books, software, etc.;
- establishing new personal contacts, professional networking, etc.;
- familiarization with another country, its institutions and their functions;
- personal development and building of self-confidence.

Gradually, internationalization is making strides in fields which were perceived as foremost national domains, such as quality assessment and accreditation. Such initiatives as Universitas 21, which is run from the University of Melbourne and which brings together a group of large but more or less similar profile public universities round the world (in Australia, Canada, New Zealand, Singapore, the United Kingdom and the United States) to accredit each other and share external examiners, will be followed by other types of global network (*Times Higher Education Supplement* 1998: 9).

Conclusions

History shows that social and economic development is rarely an outcome of one, however powerful, factor or encompassing concept, and 'globalization' is only one such factor. There are several others which are no less important or less complex. UNESCO's *Policy Paper for Change and Development in Higher Education* (1995) identifies, in addition to globalization, several other trends which are directly or indirectly shaping the development of HE. These are:

- Democratization, which brought about the collapse of many totalitarian regimes, the steady advance of democratic forces, the development of civil society and progress in the respect for human rights.
- Regionalization, as groups of states associate themselves in order to facilitate trade and economic integration. The other form of regionalization is that within existing states. All these regional arrangements are also making inroads in matters of education, culture, scientific cooperation and academic labour markets.
- Polarization of inequalities, resulting in a widening gap between rich and poor countries and within the various categories of society.
- Marginalization and fragmentation, which, due to various forms of underdevelopment, foment social and cultural exclusion and divide whole communities along ethnic, tribal or religious lines (UNESCO 1995).

Globalization is a relatively new phenomenon and some of its processes are just beginning to show at local, national and international levels. We have only just started to organize our international life in a way which will allow us to deal with the problems associated with this multi-faceted phenomenon. Globalization does not have to be seen as a downward-pointed mega-design threatening cultural diversity or insatiable globalized commercialism. It is true that it can reduce local and national sovereignty particularly in economic and financial areas. But it can work to the advantage of social and economic development in many developing countries and disadvantaged groups in our society. It might help us to understand and accept that the world continues to undergo immense transformations and is beset by problems which can and must be dealt with on a worldwide basis. It brings much closer to our collective attention, through traditional media, satellite television and Internet-based networks, what is going on in the world.

As in the past, HE is going to be involved in searching for a response to the above challenges not least because universities and other HE and academic institutions have become central in modern society and their role has shifted from being a *reflection* of social, cultural and economic relationships to being a *determinant* of such relationships. This will only be reinforced by an advancement of science and its growing role in our biological, economic and social lives.

The frank acknowledgement that globalization has become a permanent feature of our social, economic and cultural space is essential in order to take advantage of what it can offer as well as to avoid the perils it may involve. I think society can expect that universities and other HE institutions will try to reflect on how globalization affects our society and its institutions. Why? Because universities are one of those places conducive to a development and gestation of theories, ideas, and innovations. Primarily through critical examination, they are enhancing our individual and collective ability for selection and application of ideas in all spheres of social, cultural, technical and economic activity. These functions of universities, without minimizing their traditionally central roles in teaching, learning, and scholarship, are important as they are one of the major determinants of how successful we are all going to be in dealing with the challenges and opportunities brought by globalization. It is the mission of global organizations like UNESCO to promote the global vision of HE in which people are enabled to function in their personal, professional and community lives, and are able to be perpetuators and repositories of knowledge, ideas and local and national cultural traditions.

References

Daniel, J. (1996) The world cuisine of borderless knowledge, *Times Higher Education Supplement*, 9 August.

Perkins, J. (1977) Four axioms and three topics of common interest in the field of higher education, *The Contribution of Higher Education in Europe to the Development of Changing Societies*. Bucharest, UNESCO/CEPES.

Times Higher Education Supplement (1998) A world wide web of elite universities, 13 March.

UNESCO (1995) *Policy Paper for Change and Development in Higher Education*. Paris, UNESCO.

UNESCO (1997) *Adult Education in a Polarizing World*. Paris, UNESCO.

World Bank (1994) *Higher Education: The Lessons of Experience*. Washington, DC, World Bank.

9

Massification, Internationalization and Globalization

Peter Scott

Two themes have run through this book, often explicitly and always implicitly. The first is the synergy, or tension, between internationalization and massification. In other words, do higher education (HE) systems and institutions have to choose between internationalist and populist missions, or can they be creatively combined? The second theme is the contrast between internationalization and globalization. Are they simply different words to describe the same process or are they, as I suspect, radically different processes dialectically opposed? These two themes, of course, are linked. Put (far too) simply, the mass university may easily be a global university and vice versa. As John Urry directly and other contributors obliquely have argued, the changing configuration of time-space, conceptually and technologically, has made it not only possible, but almost compulsory, to combine the local and the global. Institutions, teachers, researchers and students can surf the world. But it may be much more difficult for a university to be both mass and international. The former demands an 'inward' orientation, widening access for underrepresented social groups and/or meeting the needs of local economies and communities, while the latter suggests an 'outward' orientation, enhancing international networks of scholars and scientists.

Massification and internationalization

The first theme can be summed up in two contrasting phrases: wider or deeper, or wider and deeper? The question is whether, as the first of these phrases suggests, there is a tension between the international mission of universities and colleges and the growth of mass HE systems inevitably more rooted in and responsive to local circumstances, or whether, as the second phrase suggests, there is a natural correspondence, even a synergy, between internationalization and massification. To put it in more concrete terms, is there is conflict between stimulating international student (and staff) mobility, encouraging international education, fostering academic collaboration with universities in other countries and such like on the one hand, and on the other widening access to HE, developing a more relevant and more modern curriculum, building stronger links between HE and both the economy and 'lower' education? Or do they fit together? Can we reach out to the disadvantaged and excluded in our own societies at the same time as reaching out across national frontiers to other systems of HE?

These are not simple questions. So there cannot be straightforward answers. Clearly there is a potential conflict between how universities sell themselves to potential overseas customers and how they sell themselves to the national politicians (who provide their budgets) and to their own citizens, whether taxpayers or students. For the first group claims of exclusivity, even élitism, are a come-on; back at home they are a turn-off. But it can also be argued that the marketing and managerial skills acquired in building up international 'business' are the same entrepreneurial skills needed in the consumer-driven environment typical of most mass HE systems. Similarly the presence of both international students and non-standard students (i.e. the new students sucked into universities by mass expansion) encourages universities to revise their courses, in terms of content and delivery, and to question the traditional discipline-bound structures that dominated the curriculum in élite higher education systems.

The first part of this chapter is divided into four sections. The first offers a historical context (perhaps rhetorical is better). Has the university, as is usually claimed, always been an international institution? In the second the defining characteristics of mass HE systems are discussed. How does the existence of these systems modify the allegedly internationalist values inherited from the university's élite past? The third section examines in more detail the various aspects of international exchange: student and staff flows between countries, institution-to-institution and nation-to-nation collaboration, the flows of science and knowledge around the world and so on. The fourth returns to the main question: wider *or* deeper or wider *and* deeper?

The myth of the international university

The university has always been regarded as inherently an international institution. Grand notions of the *studia generales* of medieval Europe, of students wandering from Bologna to Paris to Oxford suggest that from its earliest times the university transcended national frontiers. But the frontiers between state, community and people, between temporal and spiritual power were very different then, more fluid and more permeable, than the frontiers of the modern world. These medieval memories are reinforced by images of the Renaissance and, two centuries later, of Enlightenment Europe (although universities as institutions played a rather secondary role in the latter movement). But these memories and images may be misleading if they are taken as proof that the university always has been, and therefore always should be, an international institution. Most universities are not ancient institutions with links that go back unbroken to the Middle Ages. Even the few that do have a pedigree stretching back across the centuries have been utterly transformed by the modern world. Most universities, whether founded by a sixteenth-century king or duke or by a nineteenth- or twentieth-century democracy, are creatures, because they are creations, of the nation state. In the United States it was the Morrill Act in the 1860s which established the land-grant universities. Today the world's greatest research universities, their original purpose was to open up the unexploited wealth of the continent, largely by fostering agricultural improvement. In Britain most universities were established to meet the needs of a developing industrial and urban society.

Today universities are more dependent than ever on national governments for their budgets. The expansion of HE in almost every country has been intimately linked with the explosive extension of the power and influence of the state since 1945. Modern systems of HE could not exist without the patronage of the national state. One, the most obvious, aspect of that patronage is financial. Public expenditure provides the bulk of HE's revenue. And, as HE has expanded and its aggregate budget has increased, the pressure has grown for greater productivity and efficiency. So governments have interfered more and more in the previously autonomous – or, at any rate, lightly policed – sphere of HE to secure the best value for money. But these trends towards ever-increasing financial dependence, and so tighter political accountability, are only half the story. Millions of tax dollars or pounds are poured into HE because politicians believe that universities fulfil certain vital national purposes. Once, these were to strengthen the military capacity of the state; hence the close embrace between universities and the state, scientists and the military in Britain in the Second World War and in the United States during the cold war. When the definitive history comes to be written, it will be shown that the massive investment in American HE between 1945 and 1980 owed a great deal to the Soviet challenge. More recently the national purposes supposedly served by HE have been concerned with economic development and, in the case of the post-colonial world, nation-building.

Rightly or wrongly politicians believe investment in HE can be translated into comparative economic advantage, a belief encouraged by theories of post-industrial society which suggest that 'knowledge' has become the primary resource in advanced economies. Both theoretical studies such as Daniel Bell's *The Coming of Post-Industrial Society* (Bell 1973) and more popular accounts such as Robert Reich's *The Work of Nations* (Reich 1992) concur that investment in scientific research and in HE has now become a key factor in international competitiveness. The instruments of international rivalry are no longer fleets and missiles but 'intellectual property', in the shape of both basic science and commercial patents, and 'human capital', in the form of highly skilled workforces. HE also still plays a key role in the creation of national identities and the reproduction of national élites. Across Africa and Asia today, as in the settler colonies and the states of Latin America in the nineteenth century, universities have been established to assert pride in new-won independence as well as to produce new indigenous élites. It is possible to treat these purposes, although rooted in national ambitions, as international in the bleak sense that they are concerned with military rivalry or economic competition between nation states. But they can hardly be described as internationalist, in the sense that they embody values that transcend national frontiers. Even in the present post-cold war age when national governments have been persuaded of the virtues of cooperation, at any rate on a regional basis, national self-interest is still dominant. Universities, to the extent that they are funded to serve these national purposes, cannot be described as international institutions.

However, it is wrong to give the impression that national governments only fund universities as instruments of international rivalry. In most developed countries HE also fulfills important social functions. As agents of social mobility universities are distributors of life-chances as well as, in partnership with the rest of the educational system, enhancing the life-chances of everyone. There are some who argue that as hierarchies based on class, race and gender become less important, new patterns of discrimination based on academic qualifications will become more influential. More radically still, in the consumer-minded societies of the late twentieth century, universities also offer lifestyles which appeal to a growing proportion of the population. Universities, therefore, are deeply engaged in issues of equity which are central to the political agenda in all democratic societies. But although it is an agenda which is common to several societies, it is difficult to regard equity as an international issue. Of course, equity is an international issue in terms of the North–South gulf between developed and developing countries. But that is very different from the form in which equity appears in the context of the university's responsibility to respond to national political imperatives.

Why does the rhetoric of internationalism play such an important part in our conception of the university? Arguably it has a weak mandate in the history of the universities and the contemporary university certainly has been firmly subordinated to serving national purposes. One, perhaps cynical, explanation is that universities have clung to this rhetoric precisely because of the inexorable and encroaching power of the nation state. It is not so much a positive statement about the university's international responsibilities but a negative statement about its actual domestic condition. And, to the extent that universities which run on high-octane internationalist rhetoric have generally been seen as prestigious and because many nations wish to possess prestigious universities, politicians have connived at the perpetuation of this myth.

So far the tension between international and national goals has been considered in terms of what Martin Trow has called the 'public life' of the university – its political and organizational characteristics (Trow 1973). But its 'private life' – the university as an intellectual institution – may be equally if not more important in relation to internationalization. It can be argued that the internationalism of the university is far more strongly expressed through its 'private life' than its 'public life'. The wandering scholar of the Middle Ages may have been replaced by the jet-setting conference-hopper, who in turn may be in the process of being superseded by the information technology revolution with its potential for teleconferencing, the stay-at-home but intercontinental conference and so on, but these are simply transitory manifestations of the same basic idea: that science and scholarship know no frontiers and the institutions most closely implicated in their production, the universities, are inescapably international. The potential tension between the university as political organization forced to pursue national agendas and the university as intellectual institution globally unbounded is suggested in the title of an article by Clark Kerr, former president of the University of California: 'The Internationalization of Learning and the Nationalization of the Purposes of Higher Education: Two "Laws of Motion" in Conflict?' (Kerr 1990).

But even this can be contested. Of course it is possible to insist on universal generalizable ideas if the Western scientific tradition is regarded as superior to all others. But the superiority of that tradition is increasingly contested by other traditions of knowledge, and also undermined by its own endemic scepticism. Even in the case of the most abstract scientific disciplines it is no longer possible to insist that 'physics is physics is physics'. Aristotle's physics, Newton's physics and Einstein's physics are really different intellectual constructions, not the same body of theories and data being progressively refined. With the social sciences, literature and history this spectre of incommensurability looms larger still. Many of the most basic ideas in economics can be reduced to ways to smooth out the onward-and-upward progress of industrial economies, because that, by and large, has been the experience of western economies since the dawn of the industrial revolution.

Equally, notions of class and functionality dominate politics and sociology, notions which no longer seem to be able to illuminate events even in the European heartland, as the sad experience of the former Yugoslavia has demonstrated. Gender and women's studies, so important in many western universities, too reflect the particular circumstances and dynamics of relations between the sexes, the labour market, the reproductive technologies, the cultural habits of our own particular kind of society. It may be arrogant to imagine that the intellectual and personal values represented in such disciplines can be universally applied. There are many more examples. Their cumulative effect is to undermine any claim by the university that, despite being in its 'public life' subservient to national purposes, in its 'private life' it espouses international, even universal, values. To build a case for the internationalism of the university on its association with the Western intellectual tradition has become (and perhaps always was) highly problematical.

Two conclusions are suggested by this analysis. First, the idea of the university as an international institution from its birth is largely a myth. Universities are national institutions created to fulfill national purposes. Second, ideas of an international community of scholars and scientists all believing in universal values is equally a myth, or perhaps an echo of an imperialist past that is better forgotten. The late twentieth-century world is complex, diverse, pluralistic. These complexities must be the starting points in considering the international dimensions of mass HE systems. Rather than trying to conjure internationalism out of past myth it is necessary to try to define it in terms of present and future conditions, the real circumstances of mass systems.

Characteristics of mass HE systems

The phrase mass HE is so widely and loosely used that it requires more exact definition. The talk is of a grand secular shift, from élite to mass HE. This shift was first obvious, and first articulated, in the United States in the 1960s. Many continental European systems began a similar transformation at about the same time but less self-consciously. Even in Britain we have become reconciled to the idea that a mass HE system is not only inevitable but desirable (Scott 1995). But, as is often the case, the more familiar a phrase becomes, the less clear its meaning. It can be defined under four broad headings.

The first of these is the relationship between mass HE systems and society and the economy. Some aspects of this changing relationship have already been briefly described, such as increasing financial dependence on the state which has fuelled demands for greater accountability and led to the closer and more exact subordination of universities to national political purposes. Two other aspects of the changing relationship between HE and its political and social environment are likely to have a significant impact on the international standing of universities. First, mass HE systems cease to be selective in any serious sense (perhaps exclusive is a better word than selective, because it is not simply a question of the ratio of applicants to places but of wider perceptions of HE's social situation). Élite systems of HE were exclusive or, rather, exclusionary. They were designed for the best and the brightest, however equitably or inequitably defined, catering for Eric Ashby's 'thin clear stream of excellence' (Ashby 1971). Mass systems are inclusive, or inclusionary. They are for (almost) everyone. Within broad social groupings HE becomes the norm. As a result the prestige and status attached to graduate status have been radically readjusted (not necessarily downwards). The second aspect is closely related to the first. The old links between HE and élite occupations inevitably and inexorably are diluted in mass systems. These links still exist, of course. Universities maintain their monopoly in the production of doctors and lawyers. But many graduates in mass systems will not occupy such privileged and prestigious roles in the labour market.

Instead they fill the ranks of middle management and staff the still swelling public bureaucracies. And, more radically still, in an age of shortening working hours and working lives, and so-called 'flexible employment', the bonds that link HE with the professional labour market become looser. For some graduates HE provides them with resources, intellectual and cultural, social and personal, which they deploy outside the context of paid work. So, in mass systems, both the inputs and outputs of HE are transformed. The result perhaps is a demystification of the university. But this 'domestic' demystification cannot remain a secret, and has a radical effect on the international dimensions of HE. No longer can it be argued – for example in support of the recruitment of overseas students – that this enables future élite to speak to future élite. Many home students no longer come from nor – and this is the big change – go to élites. Nor can it be so persuasively argued, as once-tight links between universities and professional job markets loosen, that communities of high-level professional interest will be created that benefit the host nation economically or strategically.

The second heading is the shape, and structure, of mass HE systems. Here the most obvious change is that the traditional university ceases to be the exclusive, or even dominant, institutional model within HE. New sectors, comprising new types of institution, are created. And, even when these new institutions are absorbed into unified national systems as has happened with both the Australian colleges of advanced education (CAEs) and the English polytechnics, their example influences the behaviour, and values, of the traditional universities (Scott 1996; Pratt 1997). Indeed their influence is probably intensified. And, in any case, mass HE systems are difficult to distinguish from post-secondary education systems. So new challenges arise, from the technical and further education sector (TAFE) in Australia or the further education sector in Britain. As a result, within mass systems, institutions which were originally designed to fulfil quite specific national needs, generally vocational and professional, and which may lack the traditional universities' internationalist rhetoric and commitment (at any rate initially) move closer to centre stage. This does not necessarily mean that the English polytechnics and Australian CAEs were, or that the German *fachhochschulen* and Dutch higher professional schools (HBOs) are, inward or parochial institutions without international standing or ambitions. This is not true. Nevertheless their growing influence has intensified that tradition of rootedness which has always been powerful in HE. Also the presence of 'non-university' institutions within mass systems, whether binary or post-binary in structure, adds to the diversity and pluralism of HE, as indeed it is designed to do. The complexity that results, however, can be regarded as complication and even confusion overseas.

The third heading is the institutions themselves. Even in strictly regulated binary systems where particular missions are allocated to particular institutions, all institutions take on multiple missions. And, because of the growing size of the student population, they also become much larger. At the same time, *pro rata* budgets shrink and those who pay for HE, whether politicians on behalf of taxpayers or individual students who are being asked increasingly to make a direct contribution, demand greater value for money. For all these reasons universities have to be managed in a new kind of way. Donnish collegiality will no longer do. Instead a cadre of professional managers must be developed. The university must now be regarded, and purposefully managed, as a large complex organization rather than being regarded as a loose-knit aggregation of incommensurable special interests and cliques of experts called faculties, departments, institutes and so on. In the context of the international dimensions of HE this is both good and bad news.

It is good news in the sense that, because universities are now managed and can generate strategic plans, their international roles and responsibilities can be incorporated in these strategic plans. In the past a coherent strategy was impossible. Policies emerged in blind response to the clash between the university's inherited internationalist rhetoric, which only in a small number of cases had been translated into an operational form, and the fees and other regulations imposed by governments, generally for short-term public expenditure reasons. Now, in theory at any rate, universities can be proactive rather than simply reactive. But it is bad news because the better managed university of today is also a more regulated institution. This may make it more difficult for bottom-up *ad hoc* initiatives to be taken in the arena of international exchanges and international education. Now these have to be approved, to see they fit into an overall institutional strategy, and, more crucially, costed to ensure they are not a drain on institutional resources. In addition, the managerial university may find it harder to present itself as an Alma Mater, to be sweetly embraced and as sweetly remembered by international students. The old élite donnish university, for all its faults, offered a beguiling intimacy that its successor finds hard to match.

The fourth and final heading in this definition of mass HE concerns the process itself. Because the student body is much more diverse (all ages, different standards of achievement, variable abilities), because a much larger student population must be taught more efficiently, because they are destined for a much wider variety of careers, because only a minority now has scholarly aptitudes and ambitions, because new subjects are constantly being introduced, generally organized round ideas of vocational relevance rather than cognitive affinity, the old informality that once marked the university curriculum can no longer be tolerated. Quality systems must be devised to reassure those alarmed about academic standards. Credit systems must be introduced to enable students to drop in and out and to chop and change courses. Explicit teaching-and-learning strategies must be introduced to make the best use of new technologies. And so on. All this has radical and irreversible consequences. No longer can HE be regarded, however utopianly, as a quasi-private exchange between teachers and students, an intimate intellectual engagement. Instead the curriculum and its delivery have had to be systematized, even industrialized. At the postgraduate level similar changes have taken place. The old-style PhD, based around the enclosed world of scholar and apprentice or professor and research team, has been superseded by reformed PhDs, taught masters and MBAs.

The implications of these changes for international education and exchange are considerable. On the one hand they appear to undermine those close tutorial and pastoral relations regarded, almost certainly anachronistically, as typical of élite universities, which students and staff from overseas found especially attractive. Oxford quadrangles, Cambridge courts, Harvard yard, even Telegraph Avenue in Berkeley or Chicago's enclosed South-Side campus – the charisma conjured up by this list was intimately related to a particular, perhaps peculiar, style of undergraduate education and graduate study. As new, more systematic curricula and modes of delivery have taken over, that charisma has been compromised and, arguably, the international appeal of universities reduced. On the other hand, such places were never typical of modern HE systems, despite efforts in the 1960s to reproduce their spirit in newly established institutions by building elegant suburban or semi-rural campuses and drafting high-minded missions. Also the new university curriculum, with its explicit goals, open structures and clear progression routes, offers new opportunities for international collaboration. It is much easier for universities in different countries to establish joint courses. Franchising deals become possible. Course credits can be accumulated and transferred across national frontiers. Qualifications can be internationalized. So can academic standards. These very considerable advantages, although imperfectly realized, far outweigh the potential loss of opportunities for incestuous exchange between cadet members of future metropolitan élites provided by the old informal patterns of undergraduate and postgraduate education.

International dimensions of mass HE

So far in the first section of this chapter two points have been made. First, the internationalist rhetoric to which traditional universities were (and are) so attached, although not entirely spurious, is much less securely supported by the historical record than is generally supposed. Universities, almost from their beginnings, were national institutions. They grew up alongside and under the protection of nation states. And the current size and influence of HE systems is closely related to their perceived capacity to fulfil national purposes in terms of strategic power, economic efficiency, social equity and so on. Second, the development of mass HE systems does not inhibit the growth of international exchanges and other links. But it does mean that these exchanges and links must be seen in a new light: mutual rather than one-way, market-driven as much as state-sponsored, multi-faceted rather than unproblematic. It is now necessary to examine the international dimensions of mass HE in more detail, concentrating in particular on four aspects.

The first is student flows which have been discussed in greater detail by David Elliott in Chapter 3 and Jan Sadlak in Chapter 8. The remarkable thing is that in most modern HE systems the proportion of international students has grown. This means that, however rapid the increase in enroll-ments among home students, the increase among international students has been more rapid still. There are several explanations for this rapid increase in overseas students. First, and perhaps most important, universities have been encouraged to adopt a much more entrepreneurial approach to the recruitment of foreign students. The latter are a market to be exploited, especially at a time when other revenue derived from public expenditure is constrained. Second, the collapse of communism has removed rival, and highly subsidized, host destinations in the former Soviet Union and Eastern Europe, although even earlier a retreat from the ideological virulence typical of the height of the cold war had already made them less attractive. African and Asian students who wish to study abroad now have to attend a Western university, although they can exercise a consumer's choice within an in-creasingly competitive market-place between different countries and, of course, between rival universities. Third, many countries, especially the newly industrializing countries of the Asian-Pacific region, have developed large would-be professional middle-classes with substantial surpluses to spend on HE. But often local provision of university-level education is inadequate to meet this growing demand. It is no accident that Malaysia, Hong Kong and Singapore are major sources of overseas students.

But it is not simply a question of increased numbers. A new kind of international student mobility is developing with distinctive features which have close affinities with the characteristics of mass HE systems. These dis-tinctive features are:

• Student flows are no longer largely determined by colonial or post-colonial links. For example, flows between Australia and Britain should be seen in terms of student exchanges between all developed countries, involving pre-eminently the United States, rather than in old fashioned terms of post-imperial or Commonwealth links. Far more significantly new regional groupings are developing. In Britain, for example, the number of other European Union (EU) students has increased sixfold in a decade, despite the fact that British universities have no financial incentive to recruit EC students. In Australia the University Mobility in Asia and the Pacific pro-gramme (UMAP) is designed to reflect the emergence of another power-ful regional grouping. There are several other examples.

• Student flows are now driven by the market rather than by the state. It is not an accident that the most popular subjects among overseas students, certainly in Britain, are business, management and accountancy. This is a marked contrast with 10 or 20 years ago when science, engineering and public administration were the most popular subjects. Two things have brought about this change. First, developed countries are less willing to offer an open-door subsidy to students from poorer countries as a form of indiscriminate aid to the Third World. Second, there has been a dramatic shift in the pattern of economic development. There is far less emphasis on big infrastructure and engineering projects, often World Bank sponsored, and far more on stimulating the business, entrepreneurial economy. Whether well or ill conceived, this shift in policy has had an important influence over international student flows.

- These flows are no longer about developed countries such as Britain importing students, and developing countries in Asia and Africa exporting them. The most vigorous flows today are between developed countries or, at any rate, developed countries and newly industrializing countries (NICs) (which, at any rate until the recent economic difficulties experienced by the East Asian economies, were becoming more difficult to tell apart). But there is another aspect of this which is even more important. Increasingly universities from developed countries are reaching out to students in developing countries by setting up local campuses, franchising the early years of their degrees to local colleges, devising collaborative programmes with indigenous universities and so on. As the world becomes a global village some 'international' students may be able to take courses in universities on the other side of the world without ever leaving home.

The second aspect of internationalization is the international flows of academic staff. Student and staff flows are linked, of course, because overseas students often form associations with their host institutions, which lead to later exchanges or visits when they have taken up academic posts. And many overseas students already have such posts back at home. But international mobility among staff is more difficult to get an overall picture of, mainly because there are no reliable statistics. Staff flows include everything from permanent relocation to short-term visits. Also new factors which encourage, or inhibit, international mobility among university staff tend to cancel each other out: cheap air travel encourages mobility on the one hand; on the other hand the information technology revolution means that academics can keep in touch with colleagues in other countries, and on other continents, and keep up to date in terms of research without spending all their time in aeroplanes. However a tentative list of trends can perhaps be suggested. First, there is a trend away from permanent relocation and long-term exchanges and towards quick-fix visits. This is partly because, in the past, permanent location was often associated with expatriates from metropolitan countries making their careers in colonial or semi-colonial environments. This, quite rightly, is no longer an acceptable or a necessary way to staff HE systems in developing countries. Now the emphasis has switched to more even-handed academic staff exchange programmes within regional blocs, like the European Union (EU). Second, most long-term movement is now in the opposite direction. Able scholars and scientists head for the world's academic heartland, usually the great research universities of the United States, and they do not come back. Third, staff mobility has increased most sharply among the 'management class'. All mass HE systems inevitably develop extensive managerial cadres, who are eager to emulate the jet-setting lifestyle of international business and are also increasingly aware of the comparative lessons that can be learnt from examining other systems facing similar challenges. Ordinary academics, on the other hand, have heavier teaching loads and small, or non-existent, travel budgets. Fourth, and closely related to the previous trend, is that old-style staff exchanges were predominantly concerned with research and scholarship. To the extent that these activities are less prominent within mass systems (in proportion not in total effort), the old arguments for academic mobility are weaker. Also a combination of the information technology revolution and the concentration of top researchers in the world's university heartland have also eroded the research-and-scholarship case for widespread staff mobility. Instead new forms of mobility are emerging, focused on teaching and institutional management.

The third aspect of internationalization is collaboration between institutions in different countries – in both research, which is hardly new, and teaching, which is a more recent phenomenon. Nowadays universities are always signing agreements with other universities. Pictures of vice-chancellors with pens poised are common. Some of these agreements cover a single issue – a joint course or a collaborative research programme; others have a more ambitious scope with universities agreeing to work together across a wide range of issues. Of course these comprehensive agreements can amount to not much more than twinned-town deals, all municipal – or, in this case, academic-pomp and little concrete substance. What is more interesting, however, is the emergence of new networks. No longer do university-to-university agreements take the form of Senate House in London presiding rather grandly and distantly over academic arrangements in far-flung parts of the empire. There has been a decisive shift from a quasi-imperial context to a regional one. Some of these regions, of course, can be very extensive. It is possible to imagine an association among universities of the Pacific Rim. Within Europe there is already a shadowy association of universities in capital cities, which have special opportunities and special problems, not least their high costs.

However, institutional collaboration is not simply a matter of bi-partisan agreements between universities. Governments, national and supra-national, are highly influential in this arena. For many years, as Ulrich Teichler showed in Chapter 7, the EU has sponsored a series of programmes designed to encourage academic collaboration, notably ERASMUS and now SOCRATES. Since the fall of communism, the (academic) EU has, in effect, been extended into Central and Eastern Europe by means of initiatives like the Tempus programme. One of the problems with this shift from the quasi-imperial to the regional is that some important parts of the world which seem to lack either strategic or economic importance, particularly in a post-cold war world, get left out. Africa is the obvious example. Better perhaps to be on the wrong end of a paternalistic network than on no network at all.

The last of the four international aspects of mass HE system is the flow of ideas, rather than people, around the world. In an important sense, of course, science certainly and arguably scholarship too are international. In a post-industrial age you can no more talk about 'national' science than about 'national' industry. All the most dynamic areas of modern society (which surely include university science) are now international in their scope. But this globalization of industry, not just high value but also high volume industry, and of science and technology has had an ambiguous effect:

- It has led to a far-reaching concentration of the capacity for industrial and scientific innovation. Just as only a few major corporations, generally sponsored by their governments, can be at the cutting edge of industrial innovation, so only a few university systems can be at the cutting edge of scientific innovation. Or so it is argued. And there are ready examples to support this thesis – the human genome project, nuclear accelerators and so on. This thesis also seems to be supported by the emergence of a superleague of world research universities, most of them inevitably in the United States.
- Globalization combined with ever more sophisticated information technology has produced, potentially at any rate, an equally radical decentralization of scientific capacity. The 'hardware' of big science may need to be concentrated in the Massachusetts Institute of Technology or Stanford University, but the 'software' can be produced anywhere. And it is not only in the computer industry directly that the balance between hardware and software is shifting in favour of the latter. Of course this can lead to an unequal division of academic labour, with the truly creative paradigm-busting science being done in North America (and, to a lesser extent, Europe) and routine science subcontracted to outworkers in the Indian subcontinent, Latin America and so on.

There may be interesting parallels between this process of concentration and decentralization on an international scale and what is happening within mass HE systems, whether binary or unified in their structure. On the one hand there is a trend to concentrate research in a limited range of universities, to produce scientific synergies and economies of scale as well as to stop the missions of other institutions being skewed. On the other hand there is also a proliferation of research, or quasi-research activities, throughout mass systems, as institutions which were once right outside HE are influenced by the 'research culture' of the old universities.

But universities are not just about science. The creation, maintenance and promotion of intellectual culture, more broadly defined, are also very much part of their mission. Mass HE systems have to go deeper and wider – deeper in the sense that they must meet the needs of social and ethnic groups underrepresented in élite systems and unfamiliar, even impatient, with the old academic culture; and wider in the sense that they must take greater account of non-Western intellectual traditions or, perhaps better, of the growing pluralism within the Western tradition. To a large extent these two processes coincide. Greater equality of opportunity, which has produced a sharp rise in participation by women in HE, has been accompanied by the spread of feminist ideas, even ideologies. Occasionally they are in conflict. Should universities put more effort into recruiting overseas students or widening access for the disadvantaged at home? Élite HE systems catered for narrow social élites and they also initiated their students into a coherent self-confident élite intellectual culture. Mass systems are very different. Just as they must cope with social pluralism, so they must confront intellectual pluralism. It may be no accident that intellectual movements like post-structuralism and post-modernism which emphasize relative rather than absolute truths, pluralism and even playfulness, have developed alongside the massification of HE. It may also be a mistake to imagine that such movements can be dismissed as degenerate phenomena confined to the humanities and social sciences. In science and technology the ideas of Thomas Kuhn and 'risk society' theories have played a similar role in promoting pluralism (Kuhn 1970; Beck 1992).

In the context of internationalization such developments produce ambiguous effects. On the one hand, they are a reflection of global complexity, an expression of a sophisticated pluralism which should make universities more genuinely 'international' in their values. On the other hand, mass systems (and post-modern universities!) present a much less self-confident face to the wider world. As a result they may be less attractive to potential overseas students and to staff from other countries. The balance sheet is difficult to draw up. It is very important to emphasize that the internationalization of HE is an intellectual as well as an administrative, financial and logistical phenomenon. Or it should be.

The question posed in the first section was 'wider *or* deeper' or 'wider *and* deeper'? Is there a conflict between globalization and massification – or are there affinities between the growth of mass HE systems and the increasingly important international role played by many universities? Two answers are possible. The first is that it all depends on which bits of mass systems are being considered. Élite universities within mass systems may have an intensified international role because of the creation of a global market-place in science and technology, because of their strategic importance in developing regional networks, and because they need the income from overseas students to make up for shortfalls in traditional sources of funding. But mass institutions, the majority, have a much more limited international role. Although not provincial or parochial, their main focus is on widening access to new kinds of home students, developing courses relevant to economic and community demands and so on.

The second answer is that, although in some important respects there is a conflict between globalization and massification (potential overseas students prefer élite universities, with ivy-clad campuses and old fashioned academic prestige, to mass universities), in other even more important respects there is an alignment, even a synergy, between the home-grown demands which have produced mass HE systems and the global imperatives that are shaping relations between different national systems. Perhaps the most obvious and the most controversial is the emphasis in both élite and mass institutions on markets.

There are elements of truth in both answers. Clearly the former polytechnics in England and CAEs in Australia have less extensive international links than the old universities – just as the *fachhochschulen* in Germany and the higher professional schools in The Netherlands are less international. But these differences will not necessarily persist. They are already being modified. Within individual institutions, élite and mass, some departments have strong international missions while others have more local preoccupations. So of the two answers the second is more plausible. It tells us much more about the dynamics of both mass HE systems and the internationalization of universities.

Internationalization or globalization?

The second question posed at the start of this chapter was whether internationalization and globalization were simply two different words to describe the same, or very similar, processes; or whether they were very different, even opposed, processes. Two points must be emphasized at the start of this discussion. First, not all universities are (particularly) international, but all universities are subject to the same processes of globalization – partly as objects, victims even, of these processes, but partly as subjects, or key agents, of globalization. Second, globalization cannot be reduced to the impact of round-the-clock round-the-globe financial markets, of leading-edge information technologies, of integrated world markets. If such a definition is adopted, globalization must inevitably be seen as a product of the 'West' or, at any rate, a movement that originates in (and, therefore, to some extent is 'owned' by) the developed world. But globalization can be given a much wider meaning – one that emphasizes the impact of global environment changes, the threat of political and social conflicts that cannot be walled off by tough immigration or asylum policies or policed by superpowers, and the growth of hybrid world cultures created by the mingling of global-brand culture and indigenous traditions. Seen in this light globalization is far from being a Western movement. And the role of universities within it also takes on new and unexpected dimensions

There are four topics relevant to the overall theme of internationalization and/or globalization. The first is the contrast between internationalism – a quality which the university has espoused from its earliest days – and globalization. The second topic is the very important changes that have taken place in HE, which are often summed up by the word massification. The third, linked to the first, is the radical shift from neo-colonial internationalization to post-colonial globalization. And the fourth and last topic is the even more radical reconfigurations of time and space in which the university, as a key institution of the knowledge society of the future, is directly implicated.

The internationalism of the university

In a rhetorical sense, as has already been discussed, internationalism has always been part of the life-world of the university. From the start it was defined as an international institution. But this internationalist rhetoric cannot be accepted at its face value. When the university first emerged as a distinctive institution in the High Middle Ages, its heartland was confined to a particular part of Europe – basically, Italy and (a bit later) Spain, France, England, the Low Countries and parts of Germany (in fact, an area similar to that part of Europe which today comprises the territory of the EU, which may not be entirely coincidental). The university also emerged into a world in which nation-states did not yet exist in a form we would recognize. In that sense the university could not be an 'international' institution. Rather it shared an archaic notion of 'universalism', within that narrow world of medieval Europe, with other institutions – the Holy Roman Empire and, of course, the Catholic Church. So the *peregrinatio academica* of the medieval scholar cannot be seen as a precursor of today's ERASMUS and SOCRATES student mobility programmes, or of junior year abroads, or of the (until recently) massive flows of international students from East Asia to Europe, the United States and Australia – any more than the debates within medieval scholasticism, or (a bit later) the ideological wars of Reformation and counter-Reformation can be compared to the global flows of information exchange in the knowledge society.

The contemporary university is the creature of the nation state not of medieval civilization. It was during the early modern period, between the Renaissance and the coming of the industrial revolution, that the university took on many of its present functions, servicing the professional needs and ideological requirements of the new nation states of Europe and later, of the world (de Ridder-Symoens 1996). It was in the nineteenth and twentieth centuries that the university acquired its identification with science and technology (although only belatedly: the university contributed little to the processes of industrialization and urbanization – the making of the modern world – until fairly late in the nineteenth century). It was even more recently, in the years after 1945 and (most decisively) 1960, that the university came to be embraced within a wider democratic movement aimed at expanding educational opportunity. The modern university, therefore, is a national and a novel institution. Three-quarters of the extant universities, even of universities in Europe, have been established since 1900; half since 1945.

Paradoxically perhaps, before it became an international institution the university had first to become a national institution – just as internationalization presupposes the existence of nation states. The internationalization of the university has taken two main forms. The first cannot be separated from the history of empire. One of the first acts of the Puritan settlers of New England was to establish Harvard College in 1638, just as it had been among the first acts of the Spanish colonial administrators to establish universities in Mexico City and Lima 70 years earlier. And so it went on for 300 or more years. Well into the twentieth century the processes of modernization and imperialism were deeply entwined (that may be one thing that Lenin got right!). Universities were established to train reliable 'native' administrators and to educate indigenous élites in the secular ways of the West. And in settler societies they were established as agents of incipient nationhood.

The second form arose from the prestige of 'objective' (and, therefore, 'universal') science from which the university belatedly benefited. Before the beginning of the nineteenth century, élite intellectual exchanges essentially bypassed the university. They were transmitted through the grand tour, scientific academies and literary salons. It was only comparatively recently that the university was able to capture these exchanges, and build a new form of internationalism based on science. And even that may have been unhealthily dependent on the ideological and technological dynamics of great-power rivalries. It may be no coincidence that the post-war golden age of the university was also the period of the cold war.

Now, at the very end of the twentieth century, the university faces a new environment – an environment in which the older neo-imperialist notions of internationalism are by no means dead but have been overlaid by new processes of globalization. And these processes, as I argued earlier, cannot simply be seen as a reiteration of the old internationalism, still dysfunctionally dominated by the West (or, at any rate, the developed world) but are now intensified by the new information (and knowledge) technologies. Globalization cannot be regarded simply as a higher form of internationalization. Instead of their relationship being seen as linear or cumulative, it may actually be dialectical. In a sense the new globalization may be the rival of the old internationalization. If this is true, the role of the university becomes more problematical. Can we argue that, however remote the connection, some kind of link can be established between the archaic 'universalism' of the earliest universities and this new globalization – because they both transcend, and are antithetical to, the dynamics of nationalism (and of internationalism as its logical extension)? It seems unlikely.

The massification of HE

The modern university has become a non-élite, even 'local' institution, although the distinction between local and global is itself becoming less and less meaningful for reasons which John Urry has already explored in Chapter 1. Furthermore, the diversity, ambiguity and volatility of the phenomena associated with globalization mean it has almost nothing in common with the 'unified subjects' of imperium, church and university. How then has the modern university changed? Is it justifiable to describe the university as essentially a non-élite and 'local' institution?

Two aspects have to be considered. The first is that the HE systems in many countries now have mass student populations. This is true in developing as well developed countries. Indeed some developed countries – Britain until recently, much of Central and Eastern Europe, and the newly industrialized nations of East Asia – have traditionally had comparatively low levels of participation, while mass participation is common in large parts of the developing world. As a result the old links between university education and the formation of national élites have been radically weakened – although, of course, élite institutions continue to exist and such links still persist within these enlarged systems of HE. There are many aspects of this shift which can only be referred to briefly in this chapter. One is that participation in HE is now included in a wider package of civic rights and democratic entitlements. Another is that the character of national élites has also changed as the entrepreneurial class has risen and the professional/public-service class has declined in importance. Both have tended to qualify the old internationalism of élite university systems. One great-power élite is no longer talking to another great-power élite; nor is the engagement between metropolitan and post-colonial élites so marked.

Other key changes in the social and economic positioning of the university have also taken place. Most universities are now seen as meeting a much broader range of national needs. The social responsibilities of HE are now more likely to be expressed in terms of their duty to accommodate students from less privileged social backgrounds (the working class) or from minority ethnic or religious groups in their own societies, rather than in terms of some post-imperial mission. Because of the growth of HE systems, their budgets have also increased, which has tended to strengthen calls not only for greater efficiency but also for greater accountability. Whether these pressures are transmitted through political or market processes is a secondary issue. It would be a mistake to interpret the pressure to recruit more international students in some countries (including Britain) as a reinforcement of internationalism. Rather it is an attempt to make good the funding gaps created by the unwillingness of First World governments to maintain public expenditure levels in the face of perceived resistance from consumerist voters, or to promote national competitiveness in global markets for knowledge and services as well as manufactured products. Overall, there is probably a tension between the massification of HE systems, which has tended to focus on domestic democratic agendas, and internationalization, which can be seen as giving priority to alien and élite agendas.

Universities are also becoming more 'local' institutions; this is the second element in the impact of massification. It is not simply that universities are now obliged to pay more attention to local students, in a geographical sense because more are mature or in mid-career or socially because they are no longer drawn from privileged social groups and/or are destined to follow élite careers. Alongside the massification of HE has gone a parallel process of democratization of knowledge, in terms of both teaching and research. A universal science built on notions of epistemological objectivity and firmly rooted methodologically in experimental and empirical techniques has been challenged by new ideas of contextualized knowledge production. Traditional canons of thought have come under increasing attack as merely representative of decaying hegemonies. More respect is now paid to 'local' knowledge traditions that reflect the social and cultural diversity of modern HE systems, at home and abroad. Nowhere have these revisionist and deconstructive agendas been more vigorously pursued than in First-World universities. As a result there is a crisis of intellectual authority that surely must compromise the international prestige of the university.

Global empires?

The potential tension between massification, and consequently democratization, on the one hand and on the other internationalization has already been discussed in the first part of this chapter. There it was discussed in terms of competition between institutional agendas – essentially, therefore, in an internal context. But it can also be addressed in a wider external context. Certainly this tension seems inescapable with regard to old-style internationalization built on neo-imperialist foundations. It may also be inescapable if globalization is seen merely as an intensification of the global-brand and high technology culture of the West. But, if globalization is interpreted in wider terms, the tension may be much less or even disappear. Instead there may be powerful synergies between democratization (or transformation) agendas within nations and (hopefully) the emergence of a more democratic world order, and between the new attention given to 'local' knowledge traditions at home and renewed respect for the diversity of human experience, and so the pluralism of global culture.

The key may be the dialectical relationship between internationalization and globalization. Internationalization reflected – and maybe still reflects – a world order dominated by nation-states. As a result it has been deeply influenced by the retreat from empire, the persistence of neo-colonial patterns of association, and the geopolitics of great-power rivalry (notably the cold war). In the context of internationalization the inequalities between rich North and poor South remain prominent, whether the intention is to ameliorate these inequalities through aid or exploit them by trade. The emphasis continues to be on strategic relationships, and HE is not an exception. The recruitment of international students, staff exchanges and partnerships between universities in different countries are all conditioned to a significant extent by this geopolitical context. To take a concrete and current example: Iraqi students in Britain are seen as presenting a security risk and, consequently, great interest is shown in their research programmes, while links with the Gulf states are strongly encouraged. However, this old 'economy' of internationalization is in decline. With the ending of the cold war Africa and Latin America have ceased to be arenas of great-power rivalry. Certainly in the case of the former neither neo-colonialist nostalgia nor internationalist altruism is probably sufficient to sustain established links.

Globalization, however, is a very different phenomenon. It reflects not only the processes of global competitiveness between, for example, the great market blocs of the United States, the EU and the east-Asian nations. It also involves intensified collaboration as a global division of labour between low-cost mass manufacture and services provision (largely, but not exclusively, centred in the poorer South) and high-value technology and innovation (located mainly in the rich North, but with some intriguing deviations), or sometimes their co-location most notably in the ex-communist bloc. The result, therefore, is not a stable world order of great powers and their allies and client states. Instead globalization implies a radical reordering of this world order as new regional blocs emerge (for example, the development of the EU owes as much to the dynamics of this new global order as to any high-minded project to recreate European civilization); as old enemies become new allies (and vice versa); and as national boundaries are rendered obsolete by the transgressive tendencies of high technology and world culture. Globalization is inescapably bound up with the emergence of a knowledge society that trades in symbolic goods, worldwide brands, images-as-commodities and scientific know-how. And, as was argued earlier, there are still wider notions of globalization embracing environmental and equity issues.

For the university all this presents a radical challenge. Universities are still locked into national contexts; most are state institutions. As a result they may be bypassed by the new currents of globalization and, more generally, of post-industrial change. Indeed they can be regarded as classic Fordist institutions still preoccupied with the large-scale production of public service, professional and business élites (despite three decades or more of massification). On the other hand, it is also possible to argue that universities can reach back into their earliest memories and construct models of transnational cooperation that can be applied to the new situation they face. They still possess global affinities and international networks which, although developed with very different (and perhaps darker) purposes in mind, may still be useful. Certainly on a regional basis these old associations can be resurrected, as they are being in Europe. Furthermore, the university at any rate has the potential to become the leading institution in the knowledge society as the primary location at which symbolic goods are, if not produced, at least conceived and designed.

Time and space

Will the university remain imprisoned in its national context or, at any rate, in an international context rooted in a declining world order of nation states, and perhaps be superseded by more fleet-footed globally-based 'knowledge' institutions; or will it be able to escape from these constraints and reinvent itself (and, even if successfully accomplished, what precisely would that mean)? This is an especially difficult question to answer because traditional notions of time and space are being radically reconfigured. John Urry has already discussed the intriguing theoretical debates about the abolition (and also manipulation) of time, the annihilation of space and their effective recombination in a single category of time-space. The technologies, communications and social technologies that are bringing this about are increasingly well understood. The spread of new global media and information products empires, like Rupert Murdoch's News Corporation or Bill Gates' Microsoft, are matters of increasing public debate and concern. 'Virtual' institutions are increasingly familiar, although little attention has been paid to whether institution is still the right word to describe such intangible and volatile entities.

It is important to consider, first, what this process of, in effect, deinstitutionalization means for the university, one of the most resilient and prominent institutions of the modern world; and second whether, even if global universities do emerge, they may be based not on existing universities but other kinds of organization. The first issue is crucial because, for all its international traditions and despite successful experiments in distance education and distributed learning, the university still has a very strong sense of place. It is a place to which students come (and from which others are excluded). Its physical presence, whether spread around a city or on a Brave New World campus, is still very powerful. And the university is more than a place; it is also a space, a relatively autonomous space protected from the transgressions of politics or the market, a space in which free inquiry and critical learning can flourish. (Although many universities are no longer like that, it remains a very powerful idea.) But perhaps in the post-industrial, post-modern, post-Fordist world in which time and space have been collapsed into a single category there is no longer room for either 'places' or 'spaces'. Perhaps the essential categories around which the modern world has been organized, like state, market or culture, are losing their significance. What, then, becomes the university?

This is not simply a theoretical question. For how will global universities, if they emerge, be governed, managed and funded? Of course, it can be argued that the traditional collegial patterns of university government may be better adapted to the network society of the future than traditional corporate bureaucracies. But there is little evidence that HE, as it is currently organized into many separate national systems (themselves sub-divided into sectors and institutions) will be able to mobilize its resources and concert its investment and product strategies to compete with the global organizations that already exist such as News Corporation and Microsoft. And how could global universities be funded? In the absence of supra-national public authorities, it could only be through commercial markets. However, not only might this lead to a suppression of the autonomous 'space' which, in the last resort, may be the university's unique selling-point, but again there is little evidence that universities as currently constituted have the degree of commercial organization required to be genuinely competitive. In the infotainment industry of the future universities will be niche providers, trading in relatively conventional academic goods and services. On that basis, very few institutions (business schools perhaps) could become global players. Most universities would lack the product width and critical mass.

What is likely to emerge? Probably not, despite the evident power of the Murdochs and Gateses, global universities designed by News Corporation or Microsoft. So long as nation states continue to subsidize HE (as, of course, they should and will), the market will not be sufficiently attractive to them. But nor are global universities likely to be simply extensions of existing universities, in which international activities have simply been given greater prominence. So perhaps the most likely outcome is a highly differentiated development – of a few world universities (or, more probably, of world-class elements within them); of networks of existing universities that trade in this global market-place while maintaining their separate national identities (rather as the countries of Europe have come together in the EU); of the growth of hybrid institutions that combine elements of universities with elements of other kinds of 'knowledge' organization (probably global corporations and perhaps through joint enterprises); of the emergence of 'virtual' universities organized along corporate lines (and perhaps by a single corporation, or a small number of analogous organizations); and, inevitably, of a few global universities on a News Corporation or Microsoft pattern. But the main conclusion is that these future arrangements cannot be simply extrapolated from present structures.

References

Ashby, E. (1971) *Any Person, Any Study: An Essay on Higher Education in the United States*. Berkeley, CA, Carnegie Commission on Higher Education.

Beck, U. (1992) *Risk Society: Towards a New Modernity*. London, Sage.

Bell, D. (1973) *The Coming of Post-Industrial Society*. London, Heinemann.

de Ridder-Symoens, H. (ed.) (1996) *A History of the University in Europe: Volume II Universities in Early Modern Europe (1500–1800)*. Cambridge, Cambridge University Press.

Kerr, C. (1990) The internationalization of learning and the nationalization of the purposes of higher education: two 'laws of motion' in conflict? *European Journal of Education*, 25: 1.

Kuhn, T. (1970) *The Structure of Scientific Revolutions* (revised edn). Chicago, Chicago University Press.

Pratt, J. (1997) *The Polytechnic Experiment 1965–1992*. Buckingham, Open University Press/SRHE.

Reich, R. (1992) *The Work of Nations: Preparing Ourselves for 21st-Century Capitalism*. New York, Vintage Books.

Scott, P. (1995) *The Meanings of Mass Higher Education*. Buckingham, Open University Press/SRHE.

Scott, P. (1996) Unified and binary systems of higher education in Europe, in A. Burgen (ed.) *Goals and Purposes of Higher Education in the 21st Century*. London, Jessica Kingsley.

Trow, M. (1973) *Problems in the Transition from Elite to Mass Higher Education*. Berkeley, CA, Carnegie Commission on Higher Education.

Index

The Society for Research into Higher Education

The Society for Research into Higher Education exists to stimulate and coordinate research into all aspects of higher education. It aims to improve the quality of higher education through the encouragement of debate and publication on issues of policy, on the organization and management of higher education institutions, and on the curriculum and teaching methods.

The Society's income is derived from subscriptions, sales of its books and journals, conference fees and grants. It receives no subsidies, and is wholly independent. Its individual members include teachers, researchers, managers and students. Its corporate members are institutions of higher education, research institutes, professional, industrial and governmental bodies. Members are not only from the UK, but from elsewhere in Europe, from America, Canada and Australasia, and it regards its international work as among its most important activities.

Under the imprint *SRHE & Open University Press*, the Society is a specialist publisher of research, having over 70 titles in print. The Editorial Board of the Society's Imprint seeks authoritative research or study in the above fields. It offers competitive royalties, a highly recognizable format in both hardback and paperback and the worldwide reputation of the Open University Press.

The Society also publishes *Studies in Higher Education* (three times a year), which is mainly concerned with academic issues, *Higher Education Quarterly* (formerly *Universities Quarterly*), mainly concerned with policy issues, *Research into Higher Education Abstracts* (three times a year), and *SRHE News* (four times a year).

The Society holds a major annual conference in December, jointly with an institution of higher education. In 1995 the topic was 'The Changing University' at Heriot-Watt University in Edinburgh. In 1996 it was 'Working in Higher Education' at University of Wales, Cardiff and in 1997, 'Beyond the First Degree' at the University of Warwick. The 1998 conference will be on the topic of globalization at the University of Lancaster.

The Society's committees, study groups and networks are run by the members. The networks at present include:

Access	Mentoring
Curriculum Development	Vocational Qualifications
Disability	Postgraduate Issues
Eastern European	Quality
Funding	Quantitative Studies
Legal Education	Student Development

Benefits to members

Individual

Individual members receive:

- *SRHE News*, the Society's publications list, conference details and other material included in mailings.
- Greatly reduced rates for *Studies in Higher Education* and *Higher Education Quarterly*.
- A 35 per cent discount on all SRHE & Open University Press publications.
- Free copies of the Precedings – commissioned papers on the theme of the Annual Conference.
- Free copies of *Research into Higher Education Abstracts*.
- Reduced rates for the annual conference.
- Extensive contacts and scope for facilitating initiatives.
- Free copies of the *Register of Members' Research Interests*.
- Membership of the Society's networks.

Corporate

Corporate members receive:

- Benefits of individual members, plus.
- Free copies of *Studies in Higher Education*.
- Unlimited copies of the Society's publications at reduced rates.
- Reduced rates for the annual conference.
- The right to submit applications for the Society's research grants.
- The right to use the Society's facility for supplying statistical HESA data for purposes of research.

Membership details: SRHE, 3 Devonshire Street, London
W1N 2BA, UK. Tel: 0171 637 2766. Fax: 0171 637 2781.
email:srhe@mailbox.ulcc.ac.uk
World Wide Web:http://www.srhe.ac.uk./srhe/
Catalogue: SRHE & Open University Press, Celtic Court,
22 Ballmoor, Buckingham MK18 1XW. Tel: 01280 823388.
Fax: 01280 823233. email:enquiries@openup.co.uk